GROWING A
CONVERSATION
with
Spirit

Nana the Wise

BALBOA.PRESS
A DIVISION OF HAY HOUSE

Balboa Press books may be ordered through booksellers or by contacting:

Balboa Press
A Division of Hay House
1663 Liberty Drive
Bloomington, IN 47403
www.balboapress.com
844-682-1282

Print information available on the last page.

ISBN: 978-1-9822-6575-5 (sc)
ISBN: 978-1-9822-6577-9 (hc)
ISBN: 978-1-9822-6576-2 (e)

Library of Congress Control Number: 2021905473

Balboa Press rev. date: 04/22/2021

CONTENTS

ACKNOWLEDGEMENTS

Special thanks to the editors of this book,
Claudia, Tobey, Garret, and Julian.
To the lovers, siblings, children, friends, and
strangers who make family along the way.
To the dogs, cats, horses, chickens, and other
critters who share their love with us.
To the many guides who show us the way.

Nancy Kristina Haas
(1953 – 2020)

A POEM

I am yellow

I immediately feel
warm and friendly.
I'm ready to go out
into the sunshine.
I bring smiles
to people's faces.
I warm the Earth.
I am
the sustenance for life.
When I come out,
people cheer,
children laugh,
dogs grin.
I feel so good
about this.

Words are powerful; on this, we can all agree. Furthermore, I am sure we can all agree that we handle words the tiniest bit differently when we read them, versus when we hear them. The words we read in books, for the sake of professionalism, are scrutinized by editors so that they are as neat as possible. What come to mind are research collections, biographies, novels, and final exam essays. This is not any of those-- it is something more intimate and precious. While grammar belongs to the royal family of the aforementioned genres, what reigns in this genre, the genre of personal thoughts and writings, is voice.

This published work is a collection of dutifully transcribed diary entries. Let us recall the title, "Growing a *Conversation* with Spirit." The words transcribed, then edited by myself and others, are not meant to be handled with analytical or critical eyes, for this is not the way we conduct *conversations*. When reading Nancy's words, I invite you to invoke her *voice*, the voice of a friend.

Spoken English is sometimes rough around the edges. So are humans. When we read this book, we should picture Nancy's kind spirit speaking to us the way a friend, a wife, a mother, a grandmother, would. If we see a word that is capitalized which we might not capitalize ourselves, we should see what the Word is, in the Majesty Nancy saw in it. These are the human writings and human sentiments of a human woman, and every little inconsequential imperfection that we spy in the written word is like a hug from someone we know in our own imperfect, rough-around-the-edges lives.

When we flip the pages, let us read with open *ears* and open hearts. We will get much more out of Nancy's light and wisdom that way.

The three times I got to be in Nancy's company, I thought the way she spoke (about anything!) was so wonderfully unique. She was certain and precise with her thoughts and opinions, but somehow still humble and warm. While I wish I was able to hear that voice more, I will always cherish the memories of it.

It is worth repeating: these are the human writings and human sentiments of a human woman, and that is precisely what makes them as precious as they are. The more you take care of these words as you read (hear), the more they will take care of you.

— Tobey Noble, Editor

A Gift Unfinished, Presented with an Open Heart Full of Love

"How did you turn out so sweet?"
*"I listened to nature and my guides and
tried to learn from the world."*

The interaction above is one of the last conversations I had with my mother in the final days before she passed over. Nancy had an inherent sweetness about her, a genuine radiance of love and light that persisted even as she was fading from her physical body. As you read her book, I invite you to imagine this collection of stories and wisdom as if it were being shared directly with you by Nana herself.

To do this, I would ask you to first ground yourself. Sit upright, if you are able, with your feet planted on the floor, hands uncrossed in your lap or on your thighs, and open your palms in recognition for what you are about to receive. Close your eyes or gaze at a neutral space and breathe deeply. As you breathe, allow yourself to fill the entire room you are in, relax and open.

Now, imagine that in the chair next to you, or beside you on the couch, Nancy is sitting. There are photos of her throughout this book, so if you do not know her, I welcome you to use those photos to guide your mind's eye. She looks upon you with the most kind and gentle eyes. They are full of love and adoration, appreciating all that you are, happy to be sharing this moment, specifically with you.

To be Seen by Nancy, to be in her presence, was to be truly held in unconditional love. Nancy could see and know the things about you that you tried to hide from others, and love you so deeply and fully not despite those things but because of them, and because of all the rest of you. She had a knack for sussing out your haecceity, your thisness, that about you which gives you your essence. She would draw out your passion and your joy, calling forth the light through your pain, and you would leave a conversation with her feeling so whole-- not for some magical quality about her, but for how Nancy invited you to think and feel about yourself.

Love is a core theme in this book. To have known Nancy while she was alive was to have known exactly what it meant to be loved deeply for all of who you are and have the potential to be. Nancy would see you in your greatness and in your despair and love you all the same.

Growing up with Nancy for a mother taught me how to love, to love myself, and how to love those around me. I hope that you, as you read the wisdom in this book, may also feel that love in your heart and dare to be brave in your surrender to love: to love yourself and really mean it. Love yourself the way Jesus loved. The way peace pilgrims love. The way your dogs love you (and most people they meet). And as you become a beacon of that love for yourself, so too might you welcome others into that loving. To show them by example how they may love themselves AND set the standard we can expect for loving each other.

Namaste Momma

Nancy in gentle conversation with an orb among the
mighty redwoods of northern California.

A GUIDED MEDITATION

Over The River And Through The Woods

A Guided Meditation by Nancy
Transcribed by Choopy

Just find your comfortable spot. I want you to: close your eyes, relax your shoulders - that's where we hold a lot of it. And just start to breathe, in through your nose. You can breathe out through your mouth or out through your nose, whichever is comfortable.

Breathing in, filling your tummy. Breathing out from your tummy, up to your nose.

Another deep breath.

And one more ...

We are going to take a quiet journey ...

Picture in your mind's eye, you're entering the doorway of an old ancient house. And you're facing a long hallway. As you step inside, it feels very comfortable. As you walk down the hallway, you notice that the pictures on either wall are illuminated. Portraits of people. As you walk down the hallway, you start to realize, midway, the light has begun to lower so the top half is in the shadow of the portraits. You continue to walk down the hallway. There's a small table at the end, with a candle. You walk up to the table, and blow out the candle.

BLOW

You turn to your left, and there are stairs winding down. You hold the rail and step down the stairs. Around in a circle and into another hall. That slopes down. You continue to walk. And you notice the portraits - now they are three-quarters in the shadows. The lights are getting dimmer ... And you continue this gentle walk. So quiet. And you see another table, and another candle. And this one is halfway burned down. You walk up to the table, and blow out the candle.

BLOW

Turn to your left. More steps, going down. Yes.

Now it's really starting to get darker. But the hallway is light enough to see, and you're walking down the slope of the hallway. And the last candle is almost extinguished. You approach it, and you blow it out.

BLOW

Now as you turn to the left and go down, it goes dooown, dooown, dooown. And the air is feeling damp on your face. And you feel the drip of water. Just a light drip, drip, drip. As you come to the bottom, you notice you're in a cave. And you walk through the cave, just enough light to see there's a raft sitting at the edge of what appears to be a small river.

The raft is so inviting. You approach it, and you want to just lie down on that raft. And you can feel how you're buoyed up, and it's gently moving, gently moving. And your body just melts into the fabric of the raft. And slowly it drifts away from the edge. The raft is slowly leaving the cave.

Ahh (exhale)

The coolness, the moisture feels so good. But now you start to feel a little warmth on your face as you're moving into the light - into the sun.

Oh, it's a beautiful day. You can hear the insects and birds as you just drift so gently along the river. You could stay there forever.

The raft slowly goes by meadows, tall meadows - lots of beautiful flowers.

SNIFF, ahh - You can smell - the blooming. *Hmm*

And the sun feels so good on your face. And the raft slowly comes, against a little shoreline. It stops. And you roll over gently, and put your feet on the edge and lift yourself out, onto the shore. You notice a path. Follow this path. As you drag your hands, you can feel the grass - the heads - feels beautiful. And you notice up ahead, are some evergreen trees, tall - pine, spruce. And you start to smell them.

SNIFF, ahh - It calls to you. You walk into that forest.

The ground has the pine needles, it's soft. The path is clear - inviting. You feel safe. And as you come to the other edge of that forest, now you're hearing some waves. You hear them splashing against the shore. You step out into a clearing. Onto a sandy shore. You walk through the sand, with your toes feeling the warm sand. You look. Ahead of you is a beautiful green blue ocean. Gentle waves, lapping. And a bit of a rock wall on the left side. It all calls to you. And against the rock wall is a lovely wooden bench. Let's go sit down and look at the beautiful ocean.

Ahh

As you're sitting there, you're suddenly aware; there's another presence. Only you know who that is. That presence has come to speak to your heart. Listen to the words, being gently spoken into your ear, and remember what they say.

You're filled with so much love and so much understanding, and the visitor slowly moves away, but you will remember what they told you.

And as you're sitting, you're aware of your breathing, you're aware of your comfort, and you're aware of your heartbeat. Heartbeat.

Thump thump, thump thump, thump thump, thump thump.

As the sound of your heartbeat continues, know that your heartbeat has joined with the community of hearts that exists around you. As one, we beat together.

Taking your newfound information, giving your blessings to the ocean, the wind, the waves, your visitor, you stand, and head back to the forest. Walking quietly, feeling calm, refreshed. The visitor spoke to your heart. To all our hearts. Our place of power, our center.

The forest is cool. We thank the forest and the trees. And all the elementals who live there for keeping everything so beautiful and clean. Walk through the fields, feeling the tall grasses, and the warmth of the sun. Walk gently down the slope, and there's your raft, and you lay back down. Again blending right in, like you belong - your spot. And you drift slowly back, back to the cave. And you're thanking the birds, the insects, the sun, and the fields. The raft and the river; and you feel the cool of the cave, and you're thanking the cave and the raft again.

As you disembark and slowly walk back towards the steps, now you find yourself going more to the right; around and around and up the steps, and you turn to the right. There's the candle - just enough to light it again. Light the candle. Walking up the slope, to the next steps to the right and around and around, there's that candle, light it again, back up the slope and pictures are getting a little clearer, things are starting to brighten up. Around to the right, up the steps, and light that candle, too. And now the pictures are almost clear, as you get to the end of the hall you see the portraits and you thank the house. You got out through the door and down the steps.

And you are back in your bodies.

Take your time ... to think about your experience. And come back when you're ready.

PROLOGUE

The person I was and the person I have become,
have an ocean of differences.
Tomorrow that ocean will be deeper and wider.

June 18th, 2008

As we find our footing on the trail, the weight of our day packs seems like we are transporting rocks instead of our drinking water and rain gear. The trail goes straight up the Andes mountains. My heart is racing and breathing is labored at the high altitude and strenuous trek. I and three other ladies close to my age and lack of fitness are in the back of a large group of people hiking to Machu Picchu. We walk 30 steps and stop and breathe for ten breaths until our hearts slow down a little. It's brutal for us. The guide is ahead playing his flute, calling us up the mountain. My husband comes back and grabs my day pack for the last quarter mile. We are on the incredible Inca Trail in Peru. We have just spent four days hiking through the Andes mountains on our way to Machu Picchu. Our highest point was a 4,000-meter mountain, Dead Woman's Pass.

When we arrive at the final summit we are at the beginning of the Sungate, which leads down to the ruins that remain of Machu Picchu. There is a mad rush to be at the Sun Temple to see the first rays of the winter solstice sunrise come through the window of the temple. I am flying down this last hill until Livos, our guide, stops us. He holds us back at the Sun Gate, at a large ceremonial rock. He explains how to hold our three cacao leaves and put our wishes on them. We give blessings to the four directions. He directs us to put our leaves and an offering of candy in the crevice of the stone wall opposite the huge rock. I wish for peace in my world and wait for the sun.

The crowd is below us at the Sun Temple. The winter sunrise will shine through a small window and illuminate a ceremonial rock within the temple. I'm wondering why our guide is holding us here, above the crowd and the temple when I hear in my mind, "You will be right where you are supposed to be at just the right time."

Odd, dense rays of smoky light are beginning to creep over the mountain. I'm watching this glorious blend of growing color and see a form beginning to take shape. The form is a radiant woman with long, flowing robes and hair that blends with the sunrise. She is moving slowly over the mountain like She is the ruler and guardian over this domain. She is all the colors of the mountain: rust, browns, and darkish blues.

As She moves toward Machu Picchu, Her robes are all around Her flowing, and yet they are the sunrise and Her energy and Her essence. Her hair blends into the robes like one complete picture. As She comes parallel to where we are standing, She pauses and looks over at us. We make eye contact. I feel Her love and approval. She has accepted our offerings. The energy is overwhelming.

As She continues on to Machu Picchu with the rays, my whole body begins to tremble, and tears flow down my cheeks. I cannot stop the tears. I feel like I am in shock. I can't seem to move or speak. Our guide quickly comes over and through my tears I try to explain what has happened. Livos takes the bandana from around his neck and gently wipes my tears. He quietly says to me, "Many strange things happen in these mountains". I knew I had just met Pachamama.

INTRODUCTION

I came into this life with incredible joy and love. My mother once told me that I was the only one of her five children who would crawl into my parents' laps, ready to love. I seemed to know what I wanted and needed and simply looked for those things without asking. I felt like an observer and everyone seemed so foreign to me. I learned how to survive by helping myself, watching others' examples and satisfying myself. My family lacked adult guidance and my school lacked educational support. Plus, it was really hard to pay attention to people when the natural world was much more interesting.

I believe my intuition and ability to see and hear spirit developed over years of living a very challenging life. I always had an incredible imagination that would allow me to entertain myself or come up with a story or poem as needed. Mnemonics were easy to make up to help me remember. For example, I wanted to remember three new bird names, so I made this mental note.

> If Mary Poppins was a bird watcher, she would say,
> *"A widgeon is not a pigeon.*
> *A spoonbill is not related to a fork.*
> *Never put a willet in a skillet.*
> *That would make you a dork!"*.

I also managed to achieve many things without finances or training. At the age of 16, I was able to show horses in jumping competitions for wealthy people, without having any training in riding or showing horses. I managed to find enough part time work to support two of my own horses. By age seventeen, I was able to travel as a self-arranged exchange student, staying 6 weeks with a family in Germany in exchange for agreeing to support the German family's daughter for 6 weeks in my parents' home.

My next adventure was putting myself through college. Again, hard work, saving money, and living in my parent's basement helped me achieve this goal with no debt. Before the age of twenty-one, I took time from college to spend six months in Taiwan learning the language and working until I earned enough money to buy a plane ticket home. I wanted to see how people lived on the other side of the world.

I managed to finish college and graduated with a degree in Special Education. For 30 years, I taught students with special needs. I loved this job. I raised three beautiful boys and had the good fortune to share our life with a daughter brought to us through foster care. I loved this job too. Prior to my diagnosis of stage 3 Ovarian cancer, I was able to hike across England from St. Bees to Robin Hood's Bay. During the seven years of chemo and remissions, I was able to hike through Scotland, Wales, and Nepal.

Nancy and her partner during their hike through Scotland, one of many great adventures during her remissions.

It was during my cancer treatments that the psychic experiences increased dramatically. When I would visit psychics for a reading, I would often receive messages for the psychic! One of my favorite stories happened in Old Sacramento, California. As my sister and I were waiting for our turn to ask a question, I heard someone in my mind say, "Tell her to please, please, please never dye her hair again!". When I asked the psychic about that, she told me a very funny story. She had an opportunity to be a guest on a television show. A few nights before the broadcast, she couldn't find an available hairdresser. She decided to dye her hair red by herself. Unfortunately, the dye colored her entire scalp and parts of her face bright red. She quickly found a very expensive salon to remove the dye and fix her hair. She said the voice talking to me was someone who seemed to constantly watch over her. I also had a sense that she and I had experienced a life together as children living and playing in a desert area. She seemed so familiar to me.

For a long time, many people, including psychics and counselors, have told me that I need to write a book. After many years of having experiences that were highly unusual but often very helpful to me, I realized that I had finally accepted who I am and I needed to share these experiences if that would help others. I went through years of doubting that what I am seeing is very real and not my imagination. How do you explain natural abilities, like: putting a rope around a horse's nose and jumping on him bareback or hearing plants tell you when they need water? One of my children once said to me, "Mom, they're going to burn you at the stake", to which I replied, "That happened in several lifetimes, but I don't believe they will do that in this lifetime!". Many young people would seek me out and share stories of seeing deceased loved ones. I had not told anyone of my experiences and yet somehow these teens knew I would understand. They wanted me to assure them that their loved ones did visit them and that is most wonderful. I am no longer afraid of being called crazy or making up stories.

Frankly, I have finally reached that wonderful state of not worrying about what people may think of me. And if you want me to tell you about that person standing behind you with their hand on your shoulder, I would be happy to do just that.

CHAPTER ONE

The Early Years ~ Imagination and Creativity

"Be ok with who you are."

Growing up poor and Catholic in a white Protestant neighborhood was very difficult. We were picked on and put down. Kids would chant in chorus for us to go away. I remember being punched hard enough by a neighbor boy that I blacked out. I never told anyone. It was clear to me that people wanted to harm me. It was difficult to make friends. We attended a local Catholic school about two miles from our home. We walked to school every day, feeling like it was ten miles. Sometimes, coming home, the neighbor kids would block my path. I don't remember what they wanted, but I know I felt very scared. I couldn't tell my parents about this abuse because they lived with their own monumental problems. I don't remember our parents talking to us about life lessons, but I do know that I learned many things from their examples.

When I try to remember parental influence into my secret world of imagination, I don't remember many interactions. My parents worked and came home. They provided the basic necessities. We had no family discussions. I learned from their example. I learned how to survive a difficult world. I learned how to research ways to achieve my goals with little or no money. Because of what I learned from my parents, I was able to achieve many things in my lifetime.

1

Little Nancy and her sister stretch their imaginations at a local fair.

At the age of twelve, I held two part-time jobs. The local vet paid me two dollars per hour to clean cages, feed, water, and hold animals for their procedures. I retrieved wild barn cats from groups of fifteen-plus cats, one by one, and was never bitten or scratched. My second job involved cleaning the home of a family friend. This wonderful woman became a second mother to me, teaching me how to cook and talking to me about my life. I was able to save most of my earnings to support a horse—my dream come true.

I spent most of my childhood playing alone in the abandoned brickyard and wooded area near our house. I learned how to use my imagination to play by myself. I was a horse galloping away or an eagle flying into the mountains. One day I saw a man riding a donkey and followed him to his farm. He was riding through my imaginary play area. His farm was on the other side of the woods. He had a mix of exotic animals: coyotes, monkeys, raccoons, as well as goats, dogs, and cats. He taught me how to help him care for these animals. I spent all of my free time on that farm. I would clean the pens and the barn. The owner laughed at me and said that a barn is supposed to be dirty. I cleared every cobweb. I was in heaven. I loved spending time on that farm. One day we gave the donkey a really bad haircut. I couldn't stop laughing. When I hopped on the donkey for a ride, he bucked me off into the gravel. I was a mass of brush burns. It was the donkey's turn to laugh.

The owner purchased a large pregnant mare, which he allowed me to ride. I was fearless. I could ride that horse anywhere. Being with horses seemed so familiar to me. When the foal was born, I cared for her, getting her used to being handled gently. I never had a riding lesson with horses. It simply made sense to me to teach her by learning how to communicate with her. I was able to put a rope around her nose and ride her bareback. We did not even own a saddle. I remember trying to stand up while she was galloping to attempt some trick riding. My sudden crash on gravel put an end to my rodeo attempt.

My beautiful farm experience came to an end when the owner's mother decided to sell everything. I found out some years later that the man had special needs and couldn't maintain the financial requirements. All I knew was that he was very kind to me. What I didn't realize was that that experience had taught me to judge people not by their intellectual abilities or appearances, but by their actions. This man allowed me to experience the wonders of loving and caring for animals. He had taken good care of his animals and taught me to extend that same kind of care. He respected me and I respected him. I was grateful for those happy years.

I was determined to be able to buy my own horse. I found work with our neighborhood vet, shoveling snow in winter and helping people clean in the summer. By the time I was sixteen years old I was able to purchase and board a horse in exchange for riding other people's horses. This was an incredible opportunity for me. The owner of this farm was a poor man with lofty ideals. He trained local kids to ride horses he had taken in to rehabilitate.

We were taught to show these horses in jumping competitions. He was hoping to resell these horses for a large profit. Since I had never had a formal riding lesson, I was only able to compete in the open jumping division, where you are not judged on your form but on the horse's ability to clear the jumps. Staying in the saddle was always my best horsemanship ability! I remember flying into the air and landing with the horse as she cleared each jump. I'm not sure I was always connected to the saddle. I also remember flying into the fence without the horse when she decided to stop in front of the jump after approaching at a full gallop.

Nancy is fearless, confident she clears the jump,
with such grace she soars.

My horse showing career ended the day I arrived to work a particularly gifted jumper. This horse had a mind of his own. "Pete" would bite us in tender places and throw his head back and give a big horse laugh. We loved him anyway. On my last day at the farm, I noticed that Pete was covered with welts. The owner said that the horse had refused to jump. I suddenly had a memory of finding my own horse with cuts all over the top of his head. When I had asked the owner how my horse had gotten those cuts he told he had "trained" him to quit throwing his head when we tried to put a halter on him. I suddenly felt sick.

The owner had been beating these animals, and I had been naive. I left the farm that day and arranged to have my horse moved to a safer place. I found out later from my vet that my horse had not received any grain. I knew the man at the previous barn had been stealing my grain for his horses. He would always send me on my way, telling me that he would feed my horse.

At the new barn, my horse put on weight and a healthy sheen to his beautiful chestnut coat. I spent many days and hours grooming and riding all over our small town. It was another perfect life. I would even ride my horse to after-school activities and tie him at the corner of the building. No one ever questioned the pile of horse poop near the school; I believe it was overlooked because we also had Amish families who occasionally came by the school in their buggies.

My career in horses helped me get through high school. Again, I didn't fit in. I remember two male teachers having a "talk" with me. They were trying to tell me how to be more feminine—like that mattered! I felt it was far more important to just be comfortable and I simply didn't have the money to spend on clothes, hair, and makeup. Plus, those external things really didn't matter to me. Maybe I should have had a talk with them on how to respect the individual instead of inducing shame in their students.

- and foster learning and creativity instead.

My best friend, Georgie, was also a horse woman. We understood each other. Her German mother made the most amazing meals. We spent nights at her house laughing and making plans with our horses. We slept under a large feather quilt with her windows open even on the coldest winter nights. I loved the European influence in her family, cuckoo clocks and kirsch knoedel, which is a dumpling with sugar on the outside and cherries inside with melted butter over the top. Oh my, it was a taste of heaven!

Georgie and I would spend hours riding our horses through the countryside. We would sneak through the local orchards and pick a peach in its prime. I don't know if the joy in eating such a sweet peach was the juices rolling down our chins or the fact that we got away with it. You can't even buy peaches like that.

As time passed, I had to make some hard decisions about keeping horses. I had two beautiful horses that were my sole financial responsibility. Donovan was a chestnut thoroughbred and Dax was a rather small grey who could jump four feet if I asked him. I knew I would need money for college, and my parents were not in a position to help me. I sold my horses and equipment. It broke my heart. Dax found a good home, but poor Donovan went to a spoiled rich kid who thought she could just take him out to run him in the field. She didn't understand about warming up and cooling down. He became lame and I never found out what happened to him.

In hindsight, I realize there were many times where I put uncomfortable realities to the back of my subconscious mind so I could pursue my goals. Now I know that I could have helped her to care for him. Whether or not she would choose to take my suggestions was out of my control. I also was extremely shy and had a lot of difficulty focusing on present realities or communicating my needs. From all the pain in my past, I had learned to hold unpleasant realities in a safe place in my subconscious mind. I thought I could only control a small portion of my life. I thought that if I spoke out, bad things would happen to me. I needed to move on into my independent life.

College was also a tough decision. I had been accepted at a local college and waited until the last minute to sign up for classes. The clerk was a bit amused that I had not been to any orientation sessions but allowed me to register on a conditional basis. Classes were very hard, and I had no social life. My peers seemed very unkind. I decided on a degree in special education. I preferred to work with a needy population, maybe because I felt like a square peg in this world of round holes and also, I knew that I had the patience for and loving acceptance of people with special needs. I had a lot of love and patience to share. I knew what it was like to be rejected by society.

Two years into college, I decided to take a break to see what another part of the world was like. Were the people any different? Were they kind to each other? I would take a semester off of college, much to my mother's dismay. She was convinced that I would never return to college. I was nineteen years old when I bought a one-way ticket to Taiwan. It was 1973 and Chiang Kai-Shek was the ruler. My goal was to find employment and earn enough money to come home. I had learned through family friends that I would be helped by a family in Taipei until I could live on my own.

When I arrived in Taipei, I noticed that this was not like an American city. I saw women with shovels and picks working on building a road. They would break up the rocks and soil and a tractor would carry everything out of the way. There was only one tractor and many women working with simple tools. I have heard from friends recently that Taipei is now a bustling modern city.

The family who met me at the airport was very kind. They took me to meet another family where I would rent a room. The people at my new home were also very kind to me but expected more rent than I was able to pay. They also made fun of American's big noses. I found a position working part time for a small private school where just about any American could work teaching English. Everyone wanted to learn how to speak English.

One of the students offered me a room in his home. I had to be very strong in asserting my boundaries. Unfortunately, he thought all American girls were promiscuous and put me out when I would not "put out". I was put out onto the street, in a strange country where I did not speak the language and very few people spoke English. It's interesting how preconceived ideas about people and cultures exist everywhere. The Chinese people would ask me if American girls wore bras, enjoyed "free sex," or knew about oral sex. I was shocked and embarrassed.

Fortuitously, I had met a Korean woman on the plane who lived in Taiwan with her Chinese husband and two children. She had given me her phone number. I found a pay phone and convinced a passerby to explain to her where I was in the city. The Korean woman brought me to her home to stay until I could find other accommodations. They were very poor. I learned to eat fish heads and rice for breakfast. Did you know that one of the tastiest parts of a fish head is the small piece right behind the eyes? Did you also know that if you are very hungry, you can learn to eat many different things that you might not even consider eating at home with a full pantry? After discovering that my new friend had every intention of getting me to marry her husband and help him get his immigration card, so she could come to the US to open a restaurant, I quickly began to look for another place to live!

I finally found a comfortable home with two female students who lived with a maid. Their parents lived in Japan and the young women had free reign of their home. It was perfect. I enjoyed exploring the city with them and learning to speak Chinese. Since every sign was in Chinese, I would ride a bus during the day to memorize the routes by heart.

I was invited on a trip to a rural area called Yeh Liu, where wonderful rock formations dotted the landscape. It was on this trip that a young Chinese man declared he was going to marry me. It was a very warm day and I noticed an area with a very inviting pool of water. Fully clothed, I dove in head first. My companions were a bit shocked as Chinese girls did not do such impetuous things. At that point, my paramour declared it would be better for him to marry a Chinese girl. My companions later confided in me that they would like to be so brave.

Back in Taipei, I concentrated on learning how to cook Chinese food and save money to return to the U.S. Six months later, I had saved enough to buy my $600 ticket home. This was back in 1972! It was December 24th when I headed back. After a long flight and a bus ride, I arrived with about four dollars in my pocket. It was good to be home. I learned that people were just people everywhere I had traveled.

I returned to college to finish my degree in Special Education. Before I found a job, I decided to get married and had two children. I spent those three happy years prior to full-time employment, learning how to garden, bake, cook, use local plants for medicine and sew our clothes. I remember making butter, butchering my chickens (only two because it was totally disgusting to kill my beloved birds!), and growing our food. I believed that I had a responsibility to learn how to support myself and my family and be self sufficient.

It was during this time that I began to have some unusual experiences. I began to see the dots and hear the voices. The dots reminded me of images being beamed aboard a spaceship. The voice told me that they wanted me. I did not know what they wanted me for, so I blocked them out and told them that I needed to learn how to function on this Earth before I could commit to something on a different plane of existence.

I also started to have many experiences of just knowing what was going to happen. I heard warnings when I was in danger. One day a voice that appeared to come from the back seat of my car, called out my name, "Nancy!". I snapped to attention. I noticed an erratic driver that would have smashed into me if I hadn't moved quickly out of the way. The spirits would also tap me on the head to get my attention. I didn't mind these little reminders, but I knew that I needed some help understanding these changes that were happening to me.

I was introduced to a group of truth seekers that included a clairvoyant. George had been a postmaster in a small town in PA. He began to have psychic experiences shortly after he retired. He had been napping on his couch when he literally saw his wife June at work. It was not a dream. When she came home, he told her what he had seen. She verified that what he said was true. He had had an out of body experience.

So, they started a meditation group. Many people from all walks of life, got together to hear George talk. The group would meditate together, sing and then eat. After eating, George would channel Katie.

George and Katie had an interesting history. Apparently, they had agreed to try and contact each other if one was in the physical world while the other was in the spiritual world. Katie had died in a skiing accident in Germany. When George channeled her, he spoke with a

German accent and Katie would ask for a glass of red wine (which George normally did not drink).

Katie had told us that she could access the Akashic records, which are all the information of humans and the cosmos. She spoke about the evolution of the soul which led to the evolution of the body. I remember information about how people would develop into what were called, "A, B, and C beings." She said we were all A beings growing into becoming B beings who had active psychic abilities. She told us that a C being would be able to walk through walls.

We were also told that as the world began to experience more storms, flooding, earthquakes and volcanic eruptions, people would develop more psychic skills. Our clairvoyant warned us that massive earthquakes and flooding would increase over time until our Earth would no longer be able to sustain our growing populations. These predictions took place about 30 years ago.

A map of a New Earth had been developed to show where disaster areas had transformed our continents into areas of much less land mass. Unfortunately, sometime during a late night, a group of men with guns and some kind of government badges broke into the house where the maps were stored, and they took everything, warning the people not to reproduce them again. It makes you wonder how many secrets our government hides from us.

What I learned from our group, was that it was normal to experience sounds, sights, and smells that others around me might not be experiencing. I let my psychic door open just a little more. I found that by paying attention to my surroundings and nature, that I was able to hear the voices of the plants and animals around me. I know when my plants are thirsty or need a new space in the sun. They whisper their needs to me.

Raising a family, working full time, and keeping a garden are enough distractions to stop us from paying attention to the little psychic nudges who would give us even more information. I'm talking about the impressions we may receive about a person right before the phone rings. When we answer the phone, the person in our thoughts is now speaking to us. Or we have a thought about a particular store to visit and find out our favorite item is on sale. We may have a feeling that a certain person is to be avoided or called. We may find out later that the person we avoided is dishonest or the person we called becomes a good friend. If we ignore these thoughts and feelings, we may find out later that we missed out on an opportunity for safety, joy, companionship or fun.

It took me a long time to learn that the more I slowed down and listened, the more I was in charge of my life. Until I was able to slow down with some meditation, I missed a lot. I missed the cues of awareness and the tender moments with my children. I was too worried, overworked myself, and ate poorly. I also didn't know much about myself. When we are over busy, we often give in to others' opinions and decisions. We strive to fit in with society, so we follow everyone else's advice.

After all, being our true unique selves makes us feel vulnerable. Will people accept us for who we are? If we are not feeling secure within ourselves, we allow others to form who we are becoming. This may feel ok for a time, but then we wonder why we are not motivated, or why we do not have any energy. Well, after we give our power to be ourselves, to others, we no longer are being ourselves. Holding on to that public acceptance image takes a lot of energy.

As long as we worry about being acceptable, we do not have the energy to simply be ourselves and pursue our dreams. We may spend endless hours in distracting activities like: video games, making or seeking big sugary desserts, talking hours on the phone, endless shopping for things we don't really need, going to every movie that has just come out, and watching TV. Some time spent in entertaining ourselves is part of a balance in our lives. We need to play.

But we also need time to go within and learn who we really are. We have that responsibility and right to grow ourselves. We know when our actions are okay for us or not okay. Remember how fleeting the joy of a new outfit or acquiring a little extra money feels great but soon that feeling is gone? Now remember how we felt when we made a meal for a homebound friend or helped a neighbor with a difficult task. The recipients' continued smiles and the warmth that fills us can last a long time.

It took me most of my life to give up worrying about what other people thought of me. I can't control what other people think. Besides, everyone has their own issues and problems to dwell on. For all I know, they are worrying about what I am thinking about them. When the day came that I realized I was not concerned about what other people thought of me, I felt so free! I also become more compassionate to the people around me. This process is ongoing, and it only took me about 50 years to figure this out! I hope these words can help you develop some awareness at a much younger age. Be ok with who you are.

CHAPTER TWO

Growing a Conversation with Spirit

*"You're not going crazy; you're just
tuned into another station"*

A Love Letter from Archangel Michael
September 5, 2014

*Here you are at an important junction in your life. You are
choosing the path of love. Your heart tells you to be at peace,
so you work hard at being at peace. Now you do know that you
don't have to work so hard to maintain peace within your life.
Peace is within you. You can feel it when you meditate. I enfold
you in my arms with the warmth that is yours. I breathe your
freshness into my being which is as much a part of you. Here
you are always welcome, here you are always safe. Come to this
place when peace is needed for I welcome you for infinity. You
have become the easement of love that connects all to the divine
creator. You are the staff of light that will lead all to the point of
love. You have learned the all-powerfulness of love and so it is.*

*Embrace the spirit of Creator God. Hold within your heart the
beginning of creation, the song of the universe that unfolds for
your delight. All creation is laid before you for your enjoyment.
Because you are the caretaker and the caregiver, you have the
breath of joy and appeal of laughter. You are the bell of awareness
and prosperity. You sound out to all. For this we applaud you.*

You have aspired to this level of spiritual height. Look deep, be at peace, know you are loved unconditionally just as you have loved and continue to love unconditionally. For this is the example others will follow. This is what is needed on this planet at this time. Continue on and know the path you have chosen, you can feel, is the same from your chart since the beginning of time. You have chosen well and will rest in the knowing.

This is your cradle, these are the arms that will hold you in your resting place forever. Peace and love, light and love, and so it is.

What a powerful letter from Archangel Michael! When I sit and meditate, I often have an urge to pick up a pen and just write. This is one of many messages I have received over the years. This letter speaks to my lack of acceptance of myself. We often are handed these messages in many forms.

I know this speaks to many people. But, why is it so hard to accept such beautiful and gracious words when they are given to us? It seems that when I ask spirit for an explanation or help, I receive incredibly profound words of wisdom. I don't know what to do with those words. It's like they are describing someone else. And yet it rings true in my own heart. How many times are we given compliments only to cast them aside not believing that we are smart, beautiful, gracious, kind or any number of wonderful qualities? What does it take to accept and believe that we are beings of the light, co-creators of our own realities and that we are capable of magnificence?

In a graduate class for Clinical Psychology, I received this kind of message in a more earthly way. It was the last day of class. I was one of the older members of the class and had tried to share some information about selecting our parents before we are born. (In other words, quit complaining about your parents, you picked them. It's in your spirit chart!) I felt that most of the students didn't quite know how to take me. I was absolutely stunned to hear one young mother say, "If I had to will my only child to someone, I would give her to Nancy!" A male student said, "I used to dislike Nancy until I realized that she is everything I have always wanted to be!" And another male student said," When Nancy hangs out her shingle, I will get in line to be one of her clients." This was said all in one day!

Many people in class were teary eyed, including the professor and me. Later the professor told me that now I could no longer deny who I am. I'm still not sure exactly what that means. But you can see how the influence of spirit is all around us trying to give us information. They really hit me on the head that day.

Nancy stands proudly with her freshly-baked cupcakes
before walking them door-to-door for the neighbors.

Over the years, I have found many answers to help me understand what the messages and psychic experiences mean. I have learned how to keep myself in God's Light and Love. I have experienced angels, archangels, departed loved one's messages and spirits of God's Light. I lost any fear and concern about being a channel for these messages. This information was not coming from me but rather from God's Light and Love. The chart that is mentioned in Michael's message, is the agreement we make in spirit before our birth with a council of wise beings, to be completed in the present incarnation. These agreements are necessary for our soul growth in this life.

But there is a time in everyone's life when we want to end or amend that agreement. I felt this need to change when I reached a point in my life where I felt like a victim. After abuse in my childhood, abuse during my first marriage and again during my second marriage, I knew something needed to change or this would be my entire life. I prayed for the strength to change myself, knowing that I cannot change the people around me. It took a really long time, it took years until I could feel my own inner strength and my own voice.

Meanwhile, I had to battle Ovarian Cancer. Now, 7 years later, I know that cancer played an important role in forcing me to sit still and to be still. This is not an easy feat for someone with a lot of hyperactivity, anxiety and attention deficit. I learned how to meditate and administer Reiki for myself and others. My meditations helped me to be still in awareness. I could see the bigger picture. It became easier to organize my thoughts. The Reiki helped me to acquire a calmness. When we are calm we are able to complete the many daily tasks and goals we put before ourselves. You know what it is like when you are distraught and then notice how many things you have forgotten that day. It only compounds our feelings of worry and frustration. And, the interesting thing is, that you can meditate 10 minutes a day to achieve helpful levels of calmness.

During my meditations, many unusual adventures took place in my mind's eye. Your mind's eye is a wonderful place to visit in meditation, whether you are sitting for a period of time with a mantra or simply daydreaming. It is in that visit to the space between our thoughts and the space between our breaths, that we discover what we are (and *that* we are).

Take a deep breath. Now let it out to the count of 6. Sit without breathing in until you feel the need to inhale. It is this space between - when you have let out your breath and yet can sit still for a few more seconds before breathing in - where we have stepped outside of our egos. During those last few seconds you may experience a calming that seems to be coming from some Divine Source. You may have an awareness of visitors observing and being close to you. This is the time when I would allow thoughts to drift in and out.

As I would sit and concentrate on my breathing, thoughts would appear that had more clarity and color in my mind's eye, than my normal thoughts. I began to discern the difference between my thoughts and information coming to me from spirit energy. When I receive an interesting thought or vision, I relax and let it flow. If I try to control these images and thoughts, they quickly arrive at a dead end. When I relax, say a prayer to God and enjoy these visions and thoughts, they continue like a story. Sometimes, during a meditation, this story would pick up where the last encounter ended. So, every day the story would continue for weeks on end.

A friend once asked me how it is that I could see these stories so clearly. This is the answer from Archangel Michael.

We would like to present to you information already in your possession, but we will help to bring it to the front of your memories. Every experience uses a vehicle for understanding and interpretation of that experience. Your hands hold a phone that channels a voice that your ears take to your brain and then back to your vocal chords. These are several vehicles for understanding and interpretation. This might be a bit oversimplified, but it gives you a visual in your mind's eye.

This is the best use of not only experience but also imagination. Your experience might help you see some of the images the person on the other phone is talking to you about, but your imagination fills in the rest of the details. Imagination is key here. Imagination is the vehicle to help you see us and to see fairies and spirits. Be still and let the images come to you.

Accept the first image. Say my name. What do you see? Someone else may see something different. That is okay. Both are correct. My energy, received by your energy, produces a form in your mind's eye. For example, a new hair cut on a friend could be described by you one way and then described by someone else totally different or somewhat differently. Trust your imagination.

What is imagination? It is that skill you all possess for play. You put images and form together, without thought or effort, the creation you choose. Now throw in love and joy with play and you have our world. As a co-creator of existence, you can bring all of this into your world as you choose. Trust yourself.

This is an ancient technique used by many in physical form at any age. You will notice that that which you create, contains elements of the law of attraction. Think about what you desire, be careful now, and it will manifest. Your imagination is endless and vital for you to create your world.

Take time to be still. Then watch as your desires become your reality. You don't have to believe, just relax and accept the *vitality and essence that is yours. **We eagerly await your next creation, for you are far more interesting to us than we might be to you.***

The idea of co-creating our reality seemed very foreign to me at one time. I assumed reality was reality and I had no control over most of my life. Over the years, I have learned how a simple shift in our awareness and thinking can help us change from frustration to joy and peace.

Remember the cliques in high school and how excluded or rejected you might have felt from time to time? Those cliques exist in adult groups as well. I remember watching a group of women as part of a support group limit their conversations to a select few women. I was not one of the accepted chosen women in their group and the old feelings of unworthiness from way back in high school reared their ugly heads.

I suddenly felt very tired of feeling this way and decided to send love and joy not only to the clique, but also to the hurt Nancy who was feeling rejected. I also offered forgiveness to all the cliques I had experienced- and forgiveness to myself who invited and experienced those negative feelings.

I immediately had a release of the old hurts. I thought of the others in a much more loving manner. My dreams began to reflect this change. Instead of the usual anxiety chases and confusion in my dreams I began to experience the joy and excitement of positive experiences. Here is one of my favorite dreams.

I am with my sister-in-law who was acting as a midwife for her daughter. We suddenly realize that the daughter is in labor and there is no one else with us nor is there time to call for help. This baby is coming now. I get ready to help her, watching tiny feet begin to emerge from her uterus. Uh-oh. I tell my sister-in-law that everything is going to be fine. Her daughter immediately gets up to go to sit on the toilet, telling me that she has to "go." I follow her, keeping my hands as close to her bottom as possible. I know this baby is going to be a slippery mess. I also know that not catching this baby carefully is simply not an option. By some miracle, the baby has turned itself around and spurts out like a slippery bar of soap! There is no sound from the infant, so I hold her upside down and pat firmly on her back. She spits out dirty liquid. I take her in my arms and she is cooing peacefully. I hold her up and exclaim, "She is a perfect baby girl!" We are both filled with so much joy.

This was not the only dream of joy in that time of my life. But you can see how a shift in my thinking and awareness carried through to my subconscious as well. Dream interpreters usually say that all parts of your dreams are parts of yourself. This may be my subconscious telling me that I am indeed "perfect." Now I know. But I may forget over time, so I will have to read my book to remind myself. It's not what we think about ourselves that counts, but how we think about ourselves. I am Love and Light because God created me. I'm ok with that.

The more I meditated, the easier it became to discern my thoughts from messages from spirit. Archangel Raphael answered a question I had within me about character flaws with the following:

You are feeling the words "character flaw" are not quite right because we are made of our Creator's Essence. And then why does a person make some choices that cause pain to others or knowingly hurt others?

Let me see if I can explain this in human terms.

A person's decisions are the sum of many considerations and experiences. You can have an action or reaction based solely on past experiences, especially when you are not putting thought into your decisions. These decisions are then the result of purely past experiences whether the experiences have been observed or experienced directly. This is why it is so important to give careful thought to every action. Think about what you are about to do. Ask yourself many questions. Is this decision for your highest good, or will it benefit someone else's highest good? Will this decision cause anyone--including myself-- harm? Take time for reflection. Remember your mistakes and missteps, for these are important lessons, put into place to help you.

Every cell in your body has memory. Even if your mind has difficulty remembering, your entire body will help you by responding in a physical way. When something is right or wrong, good or bad, you will indeed have a physical reaction if you take the time to give your potential action a bit of thought. For example, when you do something that is going to have favorable consequences, does it feel good? And when you are about to do something that you suspect or feel will have unfavorable consequences for anyone, does this not leave you with a feeling somewhere in your body, usually in your stomach, that does not feel good? So how does one rein in the behavior that would have negative consequences? By giving thought before action you have more control of your behavior. Be an observer. Be an observer of yourself.

No, your characters do not have flaws, it is your ability or inability, willingness or unwillingness to make conscious choices. Your character is one of your many layers. Your character may include softness or impatience, pretense or genuineness.

Many of you live in a state of not being quite awake. This is often the result of trauma. Too many intense experiences too soon, will shut down your ability to experience because you close off when life is too painful. Iron out your wrinkles slowly. Learn to trust again.

Another question I had for Spirit was about Christmas. One of my adult sons had asked me about the true meaning of Christmas. I had only known Christmas from a childhood of Catholicism and what I saw on TV and the stores. Everyone seemed to celebrate with gifts I could not afford and lavish decorations. I was made aware of our poverty at a young age. Our family enjoyed large oranges and knee socks for gifts. As children, we were not encouraged to make or bake things. In my adult years, I was delighted to learn about community celebrations, friends gatherings where we shared our homemade jams and cookies and a season of love reminders. In one meditation, I asked Jesus how to explain Christmas to my adult children. This is what I received.

The Christmas message is pure. All Christed Beings will teach you to love each other. This time of your year is a reminder to love each other. The Native Americans also taught you to love Mother Earth. All of these messages are pure. Unfortunately, at times, people have altered the message to suit selfish purposes. The pureness is gone from earlier times. If you meditate and pray on the pure message, that of love, the spiritual awareness will help you to hear the true message once again. In this you will find the meaning of Christmas.

Since receiving that simple message, I find Christmas joy in cooking for my family and sharing time together to laugh and tell family stories. There is no stress of finding the perfect gift or putting up the perfect decorations. We don't really have a ritual other than to just be together around a fireplace with a hammock hanging nearby.

The biggest request from the grandchildren is to keep the fireplace burning, and to help them into the hanging hammock.

Since I began to listen to spirit, not only can I discern spirit messages from my own thoughts, but I have also learned many things to enhance the quality of my life. Listening is the first step to many ways of learning. Listen and observe. Take time to be still. Breathe.

Now my horses are calling for some attention, so I will return to this tomorrow.

I want to share something about keeping ourselves in God's Light and Love. I believe we have a choice at every moment to choose our thoughts and actions. This takes pause and awareness. It is not easy for me to stay grounded in my thoughts in a chaotic world. Again, meditation helps to stay aware. My favorite time to meditate is the wee hours between 3:00 and 4:30 AM. Some mornings I really don't want to get out of bed, but spirit has a way of getting my attention until I finally climb out of bed and go into my office. I feel much closer to spirit during those hours. And, surprisingly, after about thirty to forty-five minutes of meditation and Reiki, I go right back to sleep. I use a daily practice of grounding and clearing, gratitude prayers and meditation.

During a period of meditation, I was reminded of the importance of clearing and grounding myself. I had forgotten my ritual clearing for a few days and found myself in a dark place during meditation. I knew something did not feel right. I immediately stopped my meditation and came back. I completed a clearing and returned to the spirit elevator.

I found myself in a very green place where trees, grass, and multitudes of people I had come to love all were. Plants and animals whose lives I had nurtured throughout my life were there. They were giving back to me. I knew at that moment that I wanted to be a healer; more than anything, I wanted to help people, animals, and our planet heal.

Many spiritual teachers have shared prayers and methods of meditation and grounding to help us make best choices for ourselves and those we would like to help. Here is the ritual I use for grounding and clearing:

Sit in a quiet and comfortable place. Get rid of all electronics. Try to let everyone in your house know that you will need a bit of solitude. Place your hands gently in your lap. Breathe deeply and slowly for a few minutes. Listen to your breathing as you inhale, pause, and exhale.

Thoughts are okay. I usually bless them and send them on I allow current concerns and joys to "visit" my thoughts only briefly. Make a conscious effort to relax your body-- especially your shoulders. I know, this is easier said than done. Try counting ten breaths very slowly. If you lose track, start over. Don't be hard on yourself. Make no judgements.

Simply close your eyes, put your hands in your lap, and breathe in very slowly, hold and breath out very slowly. This would be count one. Continue to count ten. Sometimes I use my fingers to keep track.

There is also an excellent, restorative rest when I count to 100. It takes me about twenty minutes to slowly count 100 deep breaths. The counting helped me practice until I could use a mantra like, "I am love and light".

Now I am ready to visualize myself in my mind's eye. I see my arms stretched out. I begin by tracing my body with love and light. I continue by filling every part of the back of my body with love and light. I flip myself around and fill all parts of the front of my body with love and light. As the body is being filled with positive energy, all negatives and disease are pushed out through my toes. I gather this "sludge" in a spiritual bucket, dig a hole in the earth, and pour the dark negatives into the hole, replacing the dirt and hanging up the bucket. This helps for protection from negative energy.

Once again, I thank my Divine Creator and continue with Reiki for myself and others. I always begin my Reiki sessions with a prayer to Creator God and a request for Archangel Michael.

"I invoke Archangel Michael and the fifth dimensional tube of light. Michael, please bring in the tube of light and place it around me in this lifetime and all lifetimes, all planetary systems and source systems, all alternate realities and parallel realities, all alternate universes and parallel universes, by the force of grace. Michael, please use the sword of light to clear me of all foreign energies, foreign patterns, and foreign entities, including mirrored images. Michael, when you have removed these structures from my body, aura, and hologram, and have placed them in the tube of light, please close it up, and take them to the fifth dimension where they may be transmuted to their highest form of light. So be it, and so it is."

When Archangel Michael has completed this process, I am placing a clear protective shield around my body and aura that cannot be penetrated except for the following: my Higher Selves of the Light, Christ Consciousness energies, and my Guides/Teachers, and Beings of the Light who are here to assist me with my Divine Mission, and love energies from all sources.

A Meditation:

I am seeing my birth backwards. I travel from my mother's womb, through the umbilical cord, through her heart and up and out of her head. I remember the soft noises in her body from the beat of her heart to the squishy sounds of her digestion. I continue to travel through the cosmos. I come to a great hall of books, the Akashic Records, where all the past, present, and future books, memories and information are stored. I notice many people searching through the books. They notice me as a visitor. I know I am supposed to come back. I will learn many things from this place. The vision is over.

I had many meditation journeys that introduced me to astral travel. Each journey showed me new areas and concepts. As I grew in my meditation practice, my journeys grew. By the time you learn to accept yourself, you will have grown tremendously. It is so helpful to take some time every day to record your thoughts, experiences and hopes. You won't realize what is happening until you go back and read the words you have journaled.

If you have begun to meditate, your meditation experiences will also grow with you. Let your curiosity guide you. My meditation experiences seemed to change as I grew in learning about myself and learning how to use the hands-on healing modality known as Reiki. Reiki is used to help diminish the suffering of others. When we help others heal, everyone, including our Earth, benefits. Since I felt a great deal of love and oneness with animals and plants around me, I wanted to help them be well. I was motivated to study Reiki for their benefit as well as mine.

In 2005, I experienced my first Reiki session.

I was lying on the Reiki table in a state of deep relaxation. I could hear a large cat purring next to me and realized this was an anonymous invisible cat! He was making his presence known to me to let me know that I am empowered. I felt courage and confidence. I walked with him in Middle Earth and felt his beautiful mane of hair around his neck. He walked beside me and watched what was in front of us and around us. He was the protector. He watched when I got into the healing waters in my meditation. I pulled him into the water with me. He did not mind, but quickly got out like most cats would.

When I told the practitioner that I believed there was the spirit of a male lion lying next to me, she told me it was time for me to consider studying Reiki. She explained that the lion was a spirit guide and he would protect me when I visited other realms in my meditations. She also said something that I found very strange: she said I had received spiritual surgery during that particular Reiki session. I remember a very metallic taste in my mouth and feeling kind of tired afterward. The Reiki practitioner told me to drink lots of water and go home and rest. I really wasn't sure of all this and I thought back to what the meditation had shown me.

When the large lion, whom I called Purr, led me to the lake, I noticed that the small lake was being fed by a waterfall. There were many large rocks around the edges of the lake. As I approached, I noticed my other animal guides: Bohpu, Ginger Blue, and baby Sonji. Baby Sonji was a young elephant who walked with the larger Bull elephant, Bohpu. They were waiting and watching at the shore by the large rocks.

A group of fairies were sitting on the rocks. They wore colorful light clothes with bare feet and slender bodies. As I stepped into the healing waters, two fairies took my hands. They led me straight to the waterfall. They positioned me under the waterfall and they opened my toes and my fingers. I felt the water gently falling on me, my head was open. The water slowly coursed into my head, down into my neck, down my arms, and down to my fingers. The water entered my bloodstream and was pumped through my veins and organs by my heart. The water picked up dirt, disease, and debris, light tumors and cancer cells, and carried them down my legs and out my open toes.

Slowly, the fairies came to close my toes, my fingers, and my head. Now the water poured down over me, cleansing my skin and the outside of my body. The fairies led me back to the shore. I was greeted by a burst of water from Bohpu's trunk and a big splash from baby Sonji. Purr and Ginger Blue just watched from the shore. All of my disease had been washed away. I was healed, cleansed and ready to ride back. I greeted my higher self, inner child and shadow self. They were much healthier looking now than when I first met them a few years ago. They were very happy to see me.

Later in 2012, this particular meditation became a regular during the worst times while dealing with cancer.

After I had my first attunement in Reiki, many strange things began to happen to me: I would feel a light tap on my head every now and then as if someone was trying to get my attention; I had visions of people needing help when I was in their presence. One day when I was in line to buy some car parts, I heard the young man in front of me order brakes for his car. I immediately saw him crushed under the weight of his car.

I knew I had a responsibility to speak up. I stopped him before he walked out of the store and asked him if he had help for this job. He looked at me strangely, so I told him what I had seen in my mind's eye. He said that he had considered asking his uncle for help and now he would definitely do that. I was a little embarrassed to face the man at the counter. I knew he had heard the conversation. As I walked over to the counter, the older man told me quietly that he believed in that "stuff." Sometimes, speaking up about strange visions is like doing a backflip off of the high diving board. I'm never sure how I'm going to land.

Meditation and Reiki seem to go hand in hand for me. This is how I started with Reiki. My fourteen-year-old son had informed me that he was going to study Reiki and get his attunements. A Reiki attunement is given by a Reiki Master and enables the student to access Universal Life Force to help heal and balance themselves or another person or animal. There are three levels in Usui Reiki and my son had completed two levels. One day I asked him to give me Reiki for a twisted ankle. He quietly put his hands on my ankle and closed his eyes. I could feel the warmth of the healing energy coming through his hands. After he finished giving me Reiki, I was surprised to feel a big difference in my ankle. The pain was gone, and I was left with a mild tenderness that felt like I had an old injury that just needed a bit of care in activity.

I completed my first two attunements that year. I continued studying until I was able to reach the Usui Master level. I used my new skills for my adopted animals.

My horses would literally put their heads in my hands for me to give them Reiki. I offered Reiki to people too. I noticed that animals responded much quicker to Reiki's healing energy. One of my chickens developed an eye infection. Since she was blind in one eye now, she could not tell where her food was. She would peck at her food an inch above the food. She was unable to reach her food with her impaired vision. Over a three-day period, I would hold her gently and offer her moist bread. I would give her Reiki as I held her. Her eye began to look more normal. She eventually recovered and was able to eat on her own. My husband began to call me, "healer of chickens"! I reminded him that the healing comes from God and I am only a channel.

I was invited into the elevator of spirit. They told me I was growing beautifully, and they had much to show me. The elevator did not just go up, but sort of sideways and up into the cosmos of vapors and colors. I was told that the beings were taking me to their home where all the angels and archangels lived. I came to the Great Hall of Books. I knew the Great Garden was nearby. They told me that this was also my home. They knew how much I enjoy a library full of books and how much I love to garden. They said that all the thoughts that a person puts together is a wonderful thing to read and they were looking forward to having my books in the library as well. I was told that I needed to continue to work on my writings and it would take a couple of years to complete these projects, but that I had the time. This brought tears to my eyes. It was incredibly touching, loving, and beautiful.

During my early Reiki years, my meditations began to change. When I meditated, I would seem to go somewhere in my mind. I met three spirit guides. Two Feathers was a tall American Indian who would call my attention to feathers on the ground when I was walking. He offered me courage and strength. Chin was an Asian man who would surround my body with herbs for healing. Do was an ethereal being who would take something out of my body, reorder it, heal it, and put it back in my body. Do wore a red garment and I could not see his face. I sensed this group of spirit beings were with me always. I also sensed that I had a lot of healing needs physically and spiritually. These beings seemed to be preparing me for something bigger.

I am resting in my kayak in the middle of the Pine Barrens in New Jersey. I needed some time alone and away from people and the bustle of my life. I had pulled my kayak into a small cove for some quiet meditation. I had an awareness of resetting my Zen clock, balancing my Yin and Yang. My three guides were apparent. I felt my being fill with spiritual water from Chin. The water had been infused with herbs that would help me with my healing. Two Feathers was giving me a light infused with strength and courage. I could feel the light traveling throughout my body like medicine in my veins. Do was reordering parts he took out of my body and placed back into my body.

Then the river spoke to me. I heard the words," Which would you rather have, people or me?"
I asked, "What do you mean?".
The river said, "Think about what people want."
And I asked, "What do you want?".
And the river said," To flow."
And I asked, "No expectations of me?".
And the river said, "No, just to flow.".

I found I could meditate just about anywhere. The trips to the Pine Barrens were among the most healing journeys I ever made. We would spend three days kayaking down the Mullica river and sleep on the soft sandy banks. I loved to create a small space for our outdoor kitchen where we could prepare food near our campfire. Sometimes at night we could hear coyotes howling while we tried to recognize constellations in the clear skies filled with stars.

I am listening to a shamanic drumming meditation. This meditation takes me to Middle Earth, where it is made known to me once again that I am more comfortable around animals than people. I am with my totem, whom I named Bohpu, a huge bull elephant with tusks. I am on his back, which smells like hay and has spiky hairs. His skin is coarse and wrinkled. I see how he was formed as my totem. I see my child's self with gray clay. I am forming Bohpu. Slowly I form his legs, his body, his ears and tail and then his trunk and tusks. Creator God breathes life into him and he trumpets joyfully and triumphantly. He is created to care for me, to take me to designated places on his back, safely through middle earth, like the healing Blue Pond of the fairies. Sometimes he lets me get off his back to go into the water and other times he takes me into the water and we play together.

I became aware of Bohpu about three years prior to this meditation. When a shamanic woman was calling up a totem for me, Bohpu was in her kitchen trumpeting wildly to get my attention. She said my totem was a macaw, but she also said an elephant had walked by her. I wasn't sure about the macaw, so I named him Gingerblue. Sometimes I see the macaw riding on Bohpu or just flying along beside the both of us. The second totem I became aware of sometime later is named Purr. He is the large male lion who made his presence known to me when I first received Reiki.

Three years later, I completed my master level for Karuna Reiki. I wanted to learn more. I felt like a child in school hungry for knowledge and understanding. I wanted to learn and feel confident in using Reiki for the benefit of people as well as animals. I also wanted to help balance and heal myself.

I found out in 2011 that I had Ovarian Cancer Stage 3B. It was during my 30th year teaching, September 2010 to June 2011, that I noticed two things: my hair was falling out, and I was tired, more tired than ever before. I retired in June 2011. I spent a lot of time hiking across our countryside to build up my stamina for a 207-mile trek across northern England. For three weeks in August and

September I walked the Wainwright Trail. I noticed that it took a lot of effort to keep up with my group and my hair was shedding a lot.

In November 2011, I noticed my stomach was growing like a pregnant woman and it seemed like my female parts were pushing out of my vagina. I began to measure my waist every day over a seven-day period and noticed I had gained 8 inches and 10 pounds in that time. I made an appointment with my physician's assistant. She gave me an internal exam and immediately sent me for an ultrasound. The ultrasound tech kept asking me when my last period was and if I could possibly be pregnant. I was 58 years old and had not had a period for over two years. I knew there was a large mass on my ovaries.

Two days later, my physician's assistant called with a recommendation to call a gyn/oncologist. She gave me the name of an oncologist and said that I should call her first. She said she was sorry with this bad news. She never used the word cancer. I met with the oncologist and was told that she could do surgery the following Wednesday. I would have to wait a week. I was apprehensive and tried not to think about anything until I had the facts.

My debulking surgery included removing both ovaries and fallopian tubes. She took many samples from the omentin and lymph nodes. There was a grapefruit-sized tumor in one ovary and a smaller tumor on the other ovary. She removed about 2 liters of fluid.

My cancer was rated a 3B. I went for six cycles of chemo every twenty-one days. I began chemo on December 15th, fifteen days after surgery. The worst part was the anti-nausea medicine. I could not focus on conversations, TV, or reading. I could not eat very much and had very restless legs. I felt like I was going insane. I told my husband that I could not do this, this chemo. My joints hurt, I was constipated, and had to focus on Reiki symbols because it felt like I was sinking into a big black hole.

My family was incredibly supportive. My husband went to doctor appointments and chemo with me. I never knew I had so many friends. They brought me love soup. It was the only thing I could eat at first. I kept walking and stretching as much as I could. I researched supplements and ABM mushrooms. My oncologist let me take whatever supplements I felt were important for me. Throughout the whole process of treatment, surgery, etc. I only cried when my joint pain reached a point where I had to take Vicodin with ibuprofen. I managed constipation with natural laxatives. I learned how to do coffee enemas. I avoided taking prescribed medicine for anxiety. I did not feel sad or frustrated.

I put my emotional energy into making goals for myself to get better. I continued to meditate and gave myself Reiki. I was bald and loved it. I did not wear wigs or scarfs. I wore hats when it was cold, but I wanted my community to love my bald head too.

One day I experienced a warm response to my bald head. My oldest son and I were on a day trip and had stopped at a rest stop. Knowing how fussy he was about his car, I took off my chemo beanie and began dusting pretzel crumbs off my car seat and out the door. People walking by had these cute little smiles on their faces. At first, I wondered why they were all smiling at me like I was a small child. Then it hit me, my bald head! I had totally forgotten that I was bald.

I did finally begin to go into remission. My CA125, the cancer marker, had started at 166 and went down to 28 and finally to 6. In April of 2012 I was pronounced NED or no evidence of disease. That was when I finally broke down and cried a little every evening for a week. It was over at least for now. I had no complications from surgery, only some neuropathy in my feet from the chemo. Cancer has given me a different body. I no longer tolerate certain foods like sugar, refined flour, caffeine, or alcohol. For a long time, I couldn't tolerate bending my wrists on bicycle handlebars. This was due to the chemo infusions in my veins. I still walked, worked on my farm, swam, and stretched as much as possible. I felt like half my energy had returned and I was incredibly happy.

I had realigned my priorities, spending less time with negative people and more time laughing, helping others, and taking care of myself, physically, mentally and spiritually. I was able to start a cancer support group for women with gynecological cancers. We received chemo in a large room where six women could be treated at the same time. Since I had always fallen asleep during chemo, and missed all the great conversations, I decided to start a support group. In three years our group of Teal Sisters has grown from three to twenty-five members.

Since the initial treatment in 2011, I have recurred five times. Each recurrence was met with significant spiritual experiences. I would wake up every morning around 4 AM. Even though I didn't want to climb out of my warm bed, I knew I needed to spend this time on meditation and Reiki. I would focus on a healing process for myself and others, asking for clearing in protection and healing. I would visualize the other person who needed healing in good health. I would visualize myself healthy. In a few minutes, I could go right back to sleep.

I found myself on the spiritual elevator. The elevator stopped relatively soon. When I stepped out I saw brilliant sunshine and it sure seemed like heaven. I saw a man who I knew was Jesus. He looked slender with jeans and a light-colored button shirt, kind of like a workingman. His hair was tied back in a ponytail. He said to me, "Make sure you plant your garden". Wow what a great message! It was only January, but I got up and gathered my gardening magazines. I knew I would order plenty of seeds for the coming spring. I had the best garden that year. I also went into remission.

The main thing I have learned about having ovarian cancer for over 7 years, is to not let this disease become my entire world. It is one platform I stand on to occasionally use my voice to help others. I learned the importance of balancing all aspects of my life. I spent some time on each area of my life: emotional, physical, mental, my relationships, getting enough sleep, eating a balanced diet including vitamins, laughing every day, playing, praying, and meditating.

Most importantly, having to sit still taught me to go inward, in meditation and prayer. Sitting still helped me to recognize and discern the difference between my thoughts and those of spirit. I heard them and saw them. They are souls who have passed from their bodies and others-- archangels, Jesus, Quan Yin, Mother Mary, and more who offer helpful information. What I see and hear is translated in my mind's eyes and ears.

The following series of meditations happened in sequence over a period of about six months.

I have learned to adventure during my meditations. I begin with deep gentle breathing while sitting in a comfortable position. I had been meditating with a mantra, the sound "Yum". It feels like I am connecting deeply with everyone. I see all of this adventure in my mind's eye.

I see myself walking through my back field on a beautiful sunny day. There are many spring grasses and tiny flowers. A large groundhog hole sits in the middle of the field. I find myself sliding into this hole from a sitting position. I am sliding slowly down a dark tube of earth. There are some tree roots and insects looking quite natural. The earth tube ends above a cliffside with large rocks protecting the opening. I drop gently to the ground and slide around the huge rocks. I see a large bird standing on the edge of the cliff in front of me. I am being invited to greet this beautiful creature. She has charcoal colored wings with a reddish tint on her neck feathers. She stands quietly while I stroke her wings and talk to her. She leans down and rubs her cheek against my cheek.

I slip down the groundhog hole and drop down next to the rocks. The large bird is present and invites me to sit on her back. We soar through the sky, over large evergreen trees and lush, marshy ponds. I am brought back just as quickly.

Next meditation:
I am with my bird friend and she invites me for another ride. This time we fly for a longer period of time and end up on the branches of a large conifer with a giant nest. There is one egg in this nest. I embrace the egg, it is someone very special.

Next meditation:
I am taken back to the nest and the egg is hatching. I watch in wonder as a fluffy chick pokes his head through the shell and looks directly at me. I hear the name, "Chaa". I stay long enough to see him get clear of his shell.

Next meditation:
I am directly in front of Chaa, who has grown enough to begin flight. We rub cheeks and I know I will return.

Next meditation:
I am next to a grown Chaa. He invites me to journey with him. We fly over the giant evergreens and ponds. I notice

teepee-like dwellings below and cooking set ups over wood fires. I believe I am seeing an indigenous people.

Next meditation:

I am flying with Chaa. He lands in the camp of the people I had seen before. They are not primitive. They just live very simply. The rocks seem to hum with a special vibration. An elderly man comes out of one of the larger teepees. He has long white hair and a long red robe. He raises his hands, fingers together, palms facing me. He indicates that we should put our palms together. I raise my hands and join him palm to palm. I can feel the energy coming from his hands. He is giving me a gift of communication. It takes some time. I ride my friend, Chaa, back to the opening to my place on Earth.

It was shortly after this meditation, that I invited a friend to take a picture of me in a grove of giant redwoods. I invited any spirit present to take a picture with me. The result is a beautiful picture with two giant orbs in it.

Next meditation:

I am underground with Chaa. He offers himself and I become him. We rub cheeks. My hands slide onto and into the feathers on his wings. My hands and arms become wings. I see through his eyes. It is quite different from human eyes. I can see much farther, and the focus of the vision has a narrow circle around it. We lift off from the cliff and glide down to the village. We land on the chief's arm. I am now human me. I am guided into the tent of the elder woman. She is lying on a cot, wearing a faded red robe. Her eyes are cloudy and yet they seem to contain the universe. She surrounds me with protection. Now she is standing, and our palms are touching. She is giving me energy that I recognize as strength and protection. I know I will need this for my next journey. I come back to the surface and balance my chakras.

I Learned something from doing Reiki on some people one night. When I touch someone, I seem to know more about them than when I first meet them. I began to give a man named Mark Reiki, and I knew immediately that he was a very special person. When I had first met him, I had felt something off with him, and yet my touch told me that his hands were made to hold children with love. Perhaps the information we get through touch goes directly to our souls, whereas the information we put together when we meet someone, goes through our experiences and our ego. Our egos tend to interpret based on our experiences and expectations. I believe the information we get when we touch somebody is not interpreted but directly received by our souls as the truth.

When I did Reiki on a woman, I knew she needed to walk in water for exercise and to eat more fiber. Another person appeared as a stiff wooden puppet and she was talking about something her neighbors were doing that she believed was cursing her. I wondered if she needed to stretch her body, her mind or her heart. She was too stiff and I felt she believed something that may not have been true. Later I found out this woman was rather unbalanced.

Today when I eat, I will give all my food to God. I am feeding God. My friend Swami Narayan, says that we are spiritual beings, part of God's energy. What we consume is also being offered to God, who would not like to be fed conscious beings that had been slaughtered violently. i.e … animals. So, this morning I offered God gluten free pancakes with applesauce and cinnamon, maple syrup and blueberries. I'm sure She loved it.

We will become what we put into our bodies and our minds. We are co-creators with God, because we create our reality. I hunger for dancing and laughter. Time to create more dancing and laughter. Once, when I was lying next to my five-year old grandson, I told him his energy felt so good and he said to me, "That's because I have good thoughts, Nana". Out of the mouth of a child came a beautiful truth.

It is important to guard our thoughts and if we are having a problem with negative thoughts, we can put them in the hands of our Creator. About a year ago, I started to notice that when I would pray for help about these negative thoughts, a pair of hands would appear in my mind's eye. Sometimes the hands are brown and sometimes they are tan. When I would visualize putting these thoughts in my Creator God's hands, the negative thoughts would be gone. Sometimes I had to do this three or four times a day. Now, the Hands just appear, and the negative thoughts are gone.

Our thoughts create energy. We are responsible for the energy we bring into the presence of others, just like we are responsible for our words and actions. At times when I was most ill and incapacitated, I could feel what the person was bringing into my presence even before they said a word. During massages, I can tell where the masseuse or masseur has gone with their thoughts. I cannot read their thoughts, but I can tell if they are feeling joy, anger, caring or worry. The person's touch will resonate their feelings, which comes from their thoughts. My favorite masseur told me that he imagines that my body is a lump of clay that he will smooth out as he works out the kinks. His massages are the best for me. He is focusing on my well-being, and I clearly feel the positive vibrations from his thoughts.

So, not only do our bodies change good food into good energy, but so do our thoughts. Now I know the importance of selecting natural foods with no processing, like fruits and veggies, grains and seafood.

I also know the importance of letting God handle my worries and concerns. I can usually figure out most answers through meditation. My awareness of my breath clears my mind, allowing more important thoughts to come into my consciousness to be addressed.

After a sixth dose of chemo, I meditated in the evening. This was during my first recurrence of ovarian cancer. I was rather sad that I had to have so much poison pumped into my body.

I sat quietly, centering on my breathing. In my mind's eye, I could see myself being invited into the elevator. There was a vapor-like entity operating the elevator. We seemed to travel upward for a much longer time than previous meditations. The elevator stopped, and the doors opened. The entity gestured to the open doors. He gave off a beautiful feeling of benign energy.

I stepped onto a land that looked like there had been a massive fire. I hesitated to continue until I heard the word "trust". I walked past burned trees and grass. When I looked back, I noticed that my footsteps were generating small new buds of growth, green and healthy. I was told that my illness had generated the opening of my God parts, which included a Light that comes from God. This Light is a continual stream that will help heal others and our planet. There would be many others that will help with this healing process. It will take lots of footprints to heal our planet.

Since that meditation, I have been told that when we give Reiki to others and ourselves, we are helping to heal our planet. This healing process occurs whenever we send love and healing or simply strive to keep our own bodies healthy.

Next meditation:

This was a lesson for me. I saw Chaa and the camp, I tried to control where I was going instead of just accepting and observing. When I landed in the camp with the elders, I was told that this was not appropriate, and I needed to go back. So, I flew back and continued just to be aware of my breath until the meditation was over. This was a valuable lesson. I needed to trust and observe in the world of Spirit.

Next Meditation:

In this meditation I took the elevator. It stopped a bit higher up. The elevator, by the way, appears to be an old-fashioned, wrought iron structure with some red velvet cushioning inside. I closed the door inside, and the outer doors closed themselves. There is no sound as the elevator moves, it is a very smooth ride. My ride stopped at a practically empty room that was dimly lit. As I stepped out, I saw a small figure sitting on the floor and realized it was me at about the age of 11. I spoke to young Nancy, she said hello to me. I told her that she had an incredible life ahead of her and she would never be alone because I would be near watching whenever she needed me. We hugged, she said "thanks". I went back to the elevator and descended. Wow, that was amazing.

Another elevator ride:

This time the elevator goes a little higher up. When I get out of the elevator, I am met by a cow whom I remember from a story of abuse that made me feel so incredibly sad. There are many animals behind her, all from situations of pain and abuse. The cow tells me that their suffering happened for a reason and I was not to feel sad for them. She told me that I needed to find out the reasons for my own suffering.

Now there's a challenge. Do we even begin to know why we suffer, or if we can decrease or stop our pain? Why is it so hard for the healer to heal herself? I know that Reiki will reduce my pain, discomfort and sadness.

In the next meditation I was with a group of friends and we were listening to a drum beat similar to our heart beats.

I see myself on a dirt road, walking along. On the side of the road, I recognize my guides. They said to me, "You will travel this road by yourself. But, we have given you special gifts. We have given you a light to see where you are going. We have given you shoes strong enough to take you for the entire journey. And we have given you music, because you are not just going to walk, you are going to dance on down this road." I woke up teary-eyed. The message felt so beautiful.

Do you ever wonder about special connections with your children and grandchildren? I was reminded the evening after this meditation. I had been to a drumming meditation in a home with a beautiful painting depicting a tree of life. Then my youngest son told me about a dream he had that night. He and I were in a large cave. The cave had a tree-of-life painting near the entrance. In the dream, I told him that I needed to join a group of people by myself. He saw that as okay and let me go. He said there were people outside of the cave, like policemen. He said the group in the cave had all whispered something to each other like a secret and suddenly we were all clapping rhythmically.

Next Meditation:
This elevator ride brought me to a land of letters and words. As I leave the elevator that has brought me here, I am given a basket to gather the letters and words that are lying on the ground and in the trees. They feel like something very special

44

in my hands. Each letter is a different color and texture. I am marveling at the beauty of each individual letter and word. I am told that even though I feel that my mind is not very sharp because of all the chemo drugs, I will always be given help to write and I need to move forward with my writings.

This idea of having help to write was explained to me in another way when I was driving. I had been on a road that I take once a week or so when going to visit my mother in another town. As I was meandering down the road, everything suddenly looked very foreign to me. I was not recognizing landmarks. I pulled over and wondered if I had lost my way. I heard a voice in my head tell me that I was indeed on the correct road, and just needed to trust that even though my thought processes were not registering familiarity with this road, there was memory in every cell of my body.

I could still drive the car, use my phone, appreciate the beauty of the countryside, and satisfy my thirst with my water bottle. The voice told me to think back about how I began this drive, then to follow the road until it began to look familiar. This made perfect sense to me and my panic was replaced with confidence and a sense of peace. In about a half mile, the road began to look familiar again and I breathed a sigh of relief.

Perhaps it was the panic and fear during the mental lapse that was really my worst enemy. But think about that. There are so many things we can still do even if our brain does have some gaps. I may forget a name, an appointment or a familiar road, but I can still ask about that name, reschedule the appointment, and travel the road again if need be. My growth and development involves an awareness of the information I am receiving from my environment, from spirit, and from my Creator God.

We can choose to block that awareness or embrace it. You can see a difference in people who embrace their awareness or reject it. The aware person will seem more comfortable with themselves and their surroundings. They will have a peace about themselves. Some may say this person is more evolved. I don't know about that. We can choose awareness at any time.

A short meditation:
The elevator seems to go on for a bit longer. I am at the highest point: the cosmos. I am told that I have arrived at Pleiades. I step into a strange, yet familiar land. The beings here use rhythms of the planet to communicate and to exist. The rhythm is like music. I don't think I have the words to describe everything here. I will ask to return to learn more about this beautiful place.

When I return for the second time, I meet a woman with dark brown skin. She is the guardian of this place. She wears a flowing white garment that is more ethereal than physical. She is round in all of her features with short, curly, dark hair. She exudes warmth and friendliness.

Just recently, in the midst of pain from tumors, discomfort from adjusting to a new chemo, and fear about not having control of my body, I could sense my friend Chaa, trying to get my attention. I sat down to meditate.

I have gone through the hole in my field to Middle Earth. I approach Chaa near the familiar big rocks. I slip my hands into his wings and my hands become his wings. He guides me up into the cosmos and further up. We fly through the Akashic records and he shows me this book on the shelves. He says to me, "We already have your book".

We continue onward to the land of the magical people. This is the place where the rocks vibrate and allow their energy to be used to help the people in many ways. We land among the tent-like dwellings. I am invited into the home of the wise elderly woman who is no longer there. I am invited to lie on her bed. Many beings visit me there, bringing healing, protection and love. I sense that my meditation will soon be interrupted. I stand and bow to everyone, thanking them. I ride my grand friend back to the opening to upper earth. He bows and flies back. I quickly ride upward, exiting the tunnel and walk through my field just in time to become alert to the interruption that indeed needed my attention.

So, what does this all mean? Perhaps Spirit is trying to tell me that it is time for me to embrace my abilities to channel the healing that comes from our Creator God.

CHAPTER THREE

Psychic Experiences

"We can't fix everything in this world, but we can help to make our own little corner a better place with more comfort and care of others and ourselves."

The more you are in the presence of people who not only accept your psychic abilities, but who also have psychic skills, the more your psychic doors will open. I don't understand how this works, but it seems like our own energies can be enhanced or blocked. I was not always ready or eager to dive into my psychic experiences.

I hear you knocking but you can't come in!

I remember the night many years ago, that I dreamt about being alone in a space where a voice from a very bright light was speaking to me. The voice said, "We want to approach you". I told that voice that I needed to keep my feet grounded on this earth and that was hard enough. Somehow, I knew that the voice was indicating that I would be involved in something spiritual.

I heard some of these things when I was awake too. Sometimes I saw forms made up of dots in the corner of the room I happened to be in. Hearing spirits is actually like having words impressed in my mind, like when you are dreaming, and someone is speaking to you, but their lips are not moving and you "hear" what they are saying kind of like telepathy.

After that dream, I closed the door to these voices, so I could concentrate on surviving on this planet. At that time, I was a young married woman with two boys. I worked a full-time job as a teacher of adolescents with special needs. My marriage was not a happy one, but my children were incredible. I struggled to be the best mother and wife I could possibly be. It was so hard. My idea of being a good mother was someone who did all the domestic stuff, worked full-time, and baked bread. Whew, this was not easy. I wish someone would have taken me by my shoulders and said, "What the heck, Nancy, set some priorities and don't worry about doing so much!"

Somehow, I survived, and decided to find out about the "other side." Who are these voices? My curiosity peaked so I began to open to learning about the spirit world. I also began to have very clear pictures in my mind when someone would be talking to me. I don't mean that I was thinking about something else, rather, I was receiving in my mind's eye pictures about what the person was telling me. A young man was telling me about his dog and I saw the dog as a white spaniel with some black spots. I described the floppy ears and constantly wagging tail. He looked at me strangely and said that was true. He said to me, "Gee, just like a TV in your mind!".

During that same day, I was having lunch with a group of women at a Reiki retreat and I asked one of the women if she ever got a lump in her throat like someone wanted to say something using her body? I had this sensation for the past few weeks and it was growing stronger. She asked me to clarify. I told her it was the same thing she was doing. She said that no one knew she was channeling. I knew not only that she was channeling, but also that someday I would channel for others. One of my newly found abilities was a certain "knowing" about other people. I didn't always trust what came into my mind, so I proceeded with caution and a prayer to God.

One of the most beautiful experiences I had with Reiki, happened when I accepted a referral from a friend. She had asked me if I would be willing to work on her friend Jack. Jack was a psychic healer at the southern end of our county. He had practiced healing for many years, helping people with herbs and advice. He was a beautiful white-haired man with a gentle smile. When I first met Jack, he was wearing a pair of gloves on a warm summer day. He told me he had been bit by a Brown Recluse spider. He said that the poison from the spider had injured his endocrine system. He wore gloves so he could keep lotion on his hands because the skin was constantly peeling and his hands were very dry. He explained that the doctors told him they could no longer help him.

Jack had asked my friend to help him find a Reiki practitioner. I agreed to help. It took about four treatments until Jack's symptoms began to clear. We became friends. One of the oddest things that happened during this friendship, was the day Jack told me he knew where I was from. I didn't ask any questions on that day, but posed the question on the following visit.

I asked him, so what's the big mystery, where am I from? He told me I was from Venus. I never pursued this idea with him, and never asked anymore questions. Well, I have no idea what being from Venus means. I do feel like a square peg trying to fit into a round hole most of the time.

Meditation and Reiki are very similar to me. When I administer Reiki, I clear my mind and concentrate on the Reiki symbols. Then I breathe deeply and bring energy for my clients' healing, be it emotional, physical, or spiritual healing. It was around this time of knowing Jack the healer, that my many psychic experiences began to occur.

While attending a Reiki share party, I met a young lady named Pam at the food table. Her friend had recently died of ovarian cancer at the tender age of 23. I sensed her friend, in spirit, standing next to me with a big smile. She was eating! She said she can eat anything now. Now, don't ask me how a spirit can eat. Obviously, I didn't see crackers floating through the air, but she was holding and eating them. She was very chatty. She had long dark hair and beautiful curves. I forgot about the people around me and just quietly listened to this happy spirit.

Maybe we connected so well because I was in my fourth year of dealing with ovarian cancer at that time and I had been through similar struggles. I know what it is like to have nausea so bad you can't do anything but lay around and lose your food in the porcelain hole and just keep losing weight until the cancer is subdued or you die. Sometimes the anti-nausea meds would make things worse. I know what it's like to have pain in your joints so bad that meds don't help and all you can do is cry, and when you cry, you get a throbbing headache! Somehow our energies meshed together like pieces in a jigsaw puzzle.

The spirit's name was Jackie. Later that evening, we sat in a circle offering channeling for our friends. When one of the psychics asked for a piece of jewelry to channel, Pam handed her a ring that Jackie, her friend in spirit, had given to her. I heard Jackie say in my mind's ear," Stop her, stop her!" The psychic told me later that it felt like Jackie was holding her mouth shut.

I asked her to hand me the ring. I knew there was a secret that she did not want anyone to know about. I would let Jackie speak through me, and she did. I closed my eyes and took a deep relaxing breath. As I held the ring, I saw Jackie tossing her mane of beautiful dark hair. She said, "Yes, I have a full head of hair now. The last time you saw me I was bald. I look beautiful and I can eat anything. It was me next to you in the car, you can talk to me anytime. Look for my perfume, when it is there, so am I.".

At this point, while I was channeling Jackie, Pam said I was freaking her out, so I asked if I should stop. She said no. Jackie asked me to ask Pam to stand up. Jackie directed me to hug her friend in a very special way, a way that was not familiar to me. She whispered in Pam's ear, "Don't forget me". All the ladies in the room were crying. Pam said that the hug was special between the two friends and that was how Jackie always hugged her.

I felt honored to channel such a beautiful presence. I was told later, how much peace this experience had given the young woman, Pam, who had lost a best friend. Now she knows that her friend is always close by. This kind of helping others is what I am hoping my gift can share with the world. We can't fix everything in this world, but we can help to make our own little corner a better place with more comfort and care of others and ourselves.

The psychic opportunities present themselves when you least expect them. I was sitting in New York City in a wheelchair during one of my more difficult chemo times. One of my sons and my husband were taking me for a long weekend to enjoy a play and dinner in NY. We were waiting outside of a restaurant when a woman approached my husband, who just happened to be in a wizard costume with his beautiful long white hair and beard. She said she needed a wizard's advice. My husband told her that he was not really a wizard but referred her to me instead. I invited her to sit on the bench next to my wheelchair. She had the most beautiful red hair and green eyes.

It was one of those perfect, warm, sunny days in August. She proceeded to tell me about two job opportunities. She said she was very confused on which job to choose. She didn't give me very many details. Somehow, I knew that she needed to make this decision within three days. I also knew that she knew which job to choose. There seemed to be some lack of confidence in her own ability to make the decision. I told her that I knew she would need to be her own boss. Her creativity would be stifled if she were not able to express her ideas in her own time and manner. I told her that she would need her office to have windows and earth colors. She asked me to elaborate. I told her the earth colors were like the Arizona red rocks with greens and yellows added. She got very excited. I told her I knew one of the jobs had an upper management person who would not give her the freedom she required. I did not know which one. Her eyes got wider. I told her to just talk about her concerns to me now. She said, "May I?" I said, "Of course"

She began to talk very excitedly about the two jobs and seemed to be getting a clearer understanding of which job she was more interested in. While she was talking to me, her husband tried to get her to leave because he said they had a train to catch. She refused, she needed to finish her reading. She actually talked more than I did. It was interesting to watch her work through her doubts and come to a conclusion for herself. It was apparent that holding space for her gave her the empowerment she needed to clear her mind and make her decision. After she finished up our impromptu reading, she thanked me profusely. I would love to know how she made out. But I never took her name and she never took mine. It was just a moment in the universe when two souls touched their energies together and balanced a need.

I learned something very important from this exchange. The idea of holding space for someone used to be very confusing to me. As I learn to stay in the present and keep an awareness of my own thoughts, I am more able to help other people express their concerns. So, I am listening carefully to everything the other person is telling me, without any judgment from me. If my own ideas and experiences from the past come to mind, I refocus on what the person is saying, giving them my complete attention.

Instead of developing a rebuttal for the person who is talking to me or sharing my personal information, I engage my curiosity about this person. As I am giving my full attention to the other person, I notice that they eventually stop talking and then comment about how good it was to talk with me, even if I have barely said a word. I needed to have this direct, firsthand experience observing positive results for holding space for someone, before understanding seeped deeper into me about the concept of "holding space."

Even if we are given explanations for certain things, experience is a much better teacher. The explanation plants the seeds for understanding. When the experience occurs, we now have a platform to relate to that experience. The base is the explanation that preceded the experience. So, just remember, when you are sharing things with your children and others, even though they might not appear to understand completely what you have told them, or if they seem to be ignoring you, you have still planted those seed-thoughts and now they have the base to help them further understand in time. Their experiences will have more meaning because they have a base of understanding.

Throughout my life, I have been called a "wild woman." Now this may have been an insult or a compliment depending on the person delivering this message. I know that I did not have a lot of fear of animals, just fear of people. I was afraid to disappoint, hurt or be rejected by others. As I learned to accept myself and my psychic skills, I have been able to express myself more freely. Perhaps these compliment/insults were the seeds I needed to realize:

You can't quiet me,
Buckle me up,
Zip me shut,
Or close me out,
Because I AM a wild woman!

The difference is, I know how to be more gracious in dealing with people, and I tend to love most people. I do not need to be believed, accepted, or the center of attention.

I love my wild, independent self. I love that I can choose my environment and friends. There are many books about loving and accepting yourself, easier said than done. I now know how important self-acceptance is. Time has been my best teacher. I am grateful that I can share what I know to be comforting words as brought to me through spirit. I am not afraid to bring comfort to people.

Nancy in repose on a warm summer day, her smile beaming,
rascality and wildness beneath the surface.

I had the lovely opportunity to volunteer at our local theater where a psychic was presenting. My job was to bring the microphone to the individuals asking questions. The speaker was able to clarify for some of the elderly guests what their deceased loved ones were intending to communicate to them. One woman smelled roses when she awoke in the morning. The speaker explained that her deceased husband was presenting her with her favorite flower. The psychic's explanations were comforting and precise for most people except for the woman who had lost her cat.

The last person to ask a question was a woman in the front row. It was clear that she was very distraught. She had lost a beloved pet and believed the cat's death was her fault because she had taken him to the vet for an inoculation. The psychic did tell her that he was not very good at reading animal spirits. He proceeded to describe a cat with a collar. She began to cry, talking about feeling responsible for her pet's death. As I held the microphone for her, I put my hand on her back to comfort her.

I could see her cat, lying on her chest at night when she was in bed and he did not have a collar. The cat clearly loved her as much as she loved her cat. The psychic could tell her no more. The group session was quickly over, and I finished my duties and headed out the door.

It was so strange that the cat owner crossed my path just as I headed to my car. She looked at me and began to cry again. She told me that the psychic had gotten everything wrong. I told her that I was aware of some of the details if she would like to hear them. She looked into my eyes and waited. I told her what I had seen and was able to describe her feline companion and added that he wanted her to know that she was not responsible for his death. I asked her if she felt any pressure where he used to lay on her chest at night and she affirmed. Her precious friend wanted her to know that he was with her every night and would be there for her when it was time for her spirit to cross over. He also said that he did not want her to be sad. She stopped crying and thanked me. I told her I was probably better at hearing animals than people.

Another wonderful and strange animal experience happened in a yoga studio. I had been invited by a friend to try a yoga class. The class was a small group of about 12 people in a comfortable setting. During the cool down session at the end of class I heard a horse say to me very clearly, "Please tell the lady with the brown hair that my feet hurt terribly." He wanted to have his shoes removed. He happened to be a brown horse with long slender legs. I wondered if he was used for dressage or jumping.

As I laid on the floor, listening to this horse send this information, I wondered who else heard it and would I have the courage to speak up. I took a breath and stood up. I asked the group if anyone had a brown horse who might be in pain. I know, sounds crazy, right? One brown-haired woman approached me and said she had been teaching the Feldenkrais Method to a woman on a brown horse. Feldenkrais is a form of physical exercise promoting balance. She also said the horse was limping.

Well, there you go. I guess you can receive thought information from animals who are still living. She did contact me later to say that the horse owner did have the horse's shoes removed for the winter. All I could think about was that the poor horse must have been in terrible pain to be sending such a clear SOS. Now I know that you might not expect to hear from living creatures, but apparently energy is energy whether it is in a life form or a spirit form. I believe that when we open to and become aware of the fact that we are all made of energy and therefore all connected in some way, we begin to experience more personal interactions with the energy around us.

Another lovely psychic experience came from a deceased pet. We adopt older dogs who need homes, to enjoy their final years running on our farm and fields. They live in the house with us and have a comfy nest of blankets in our laundry room. Since we tend to adopt dogs who are five to seven years old, we may only have them for a few years.

Sadie was a fun chocolate lab who would dance with me when I put music on at night. She was always so happy. We lost her after a brief three year stay with us. A few days after she was gone, I noticed a large, bright orb where her blanket nest was. I was working at the kitchen sink with a direct view into the laundry room.

My three-year-old grandson was playing next to me. I often wondered why no one else ever saw the spirits and orbs. My grandson pointed at the doggy nest and said, "What's that, Nana?". He took a few steps back. It seemed to frighten him. I knew he was seeing the ball of energy. I told him it was a doggy angel and it would soon be gone. I often notice orbs in the pictures of my grandchildren as they play, dancing along with the children.

After the orb was gone Silas asked me, "Where did it go?". I told him that it went back to Heaven but might visit us again. He walked over to a poster of a Renaissance angel that hung above my dining room table and said the word, "Angel". I told him that yes, both are angels, that angels can show themselves in many forms. At the age of six he no longer remembers seeing the orb, but I'll never forget it. His sighting confirmed to me that something was indeed there.

One of my most memorable psychic experiences happened on a vacation in Vermont. My experience with the bed and breakfast owner was otherworldly. We stayed in a lovely country home for a week during the fall to admire all the beautiful leaf color changes. The owner, Lisa, complained of a two-week long migraine. My husband volunteered my Reiki services. It's always nice to be with someone who believes in your abilities even more than you might believe in yourself.

The Reiki cured her headache and it did not return the entire week we were there. Lisa made us a couple of wonderful suppers to repay the Reiki and to make sure I had a good meal. She also invited us to a tribal dance in the community center near Burlington. It was a wonderful dancing experience. People just danced around the gym, occasionally holding each other but mostly dancing alone. One woman gathered me in her arms and held me to her gently. I felt like I was in my mother's arms. It was such a beautiful experience.

The next morning, I started to receive images and words from a man who said he was David, Lisa's father. He showed me a letter and a pair of boots. He said he was proud of his daughter for speaking her truth. He was also proud of her for having the courage to send this letter to him.

Lisa said she had written to tell him prior to his passing, about all the things that she was not happy about with him. She seemed to feel bad about this letter. She broke down in tears, talking about that difficult time of her life. But her father was showing me the letter and expressing that he felt this letter was written from a place of strength and not shame.

He also showed me a pair of brown work boots. He communicated that she was the one of her three sisters to do the "walking", or to take action to make her life better. Lisa had had a series of unfortunate events over a years' time, beloved pets dying and a difficult separation. When I gave Lisa this information she said, "Why did you come here?"

Why indeed! I seem to be exactly where I need to be. There really is no answer except that God placed me there. I gave Lisa Reiki again, before I left, and she asked to give me healing in return. I was still suffering from the effects of recent chemo, a bald head, weakness and tender stomach. She asked me to lie down beside her and wrap myself around her. We held that beautiful healing embrace for about ten minutes. It was a beautiful exchange of love and healing energy.

The day we left, a retreat center in Sedona, Arizona called to offer her a job. Lisa told the woman about a guest channeling her father and the work boots. Lisa had actually lost a pair of boots. The woman on the phone asked Lisa her shoe size and then said that someone had left a pair of boots at the retreat and they were just her size! Lisa has written to tell us that her life has changed. She accepted the job and fell in love with Sedona. She has had many wonderful adventures in the past two years and is much happier.

Sometimes psychic experiences occur when I least expect them. I was on a plane, traveling alone. A large man shared the row I was in with an empty seat between us. He never spoke to me, but I noticed he watched me out of the corner of his eye. I had received a deck of animal cards and was examining each one. The cards were a gift from my sister. A few months prior, I had a sacral cranial worker tell me that I should get a deck of animal cards. When spirit is trying to help you, they will put messages in your path in many forms. They could call your attention to a sign, something on TV or just a passing comment. I always wanted a deck of animal cards. I felt that my natural closeness to animals would help me interpret the cards for guidance and inspiration. When I was visiting my sister in Davis, CA, she said she wanted to offer me a gift from a box of new books. In the middle of the books was, what else, but a deck of animal cards! Spirit had spoken.

I felt the calling to use my new deck for the man sitting next to me. Golly gee! He was a complete stranger. What the heck was I going to say? The man got up to use the restroom. I informed whoever was encouraging me that after the man came back, if he seemed interested, I would offer a reading. When the man came back, he pretty much looked directly at me. So, I told him about the cards and asked if he would like a reading. He said he was very interested but too shy to ask. We spoke very little.

He drew the falcon card. This card spoke to him directly. He was being told to jump into his next adventure unequivocally, meaning without hesitation. I sensed he was feeling some conflicts about his destination's purpose. He began to talk. First, he asked me if I had "gone through his stuff." I had to laugh. I told him I didn't see any "stuff" and sure, in the two minutes he was gone I pulled out his overhead bag and examined each item carefully! NOT! He laughed.

He said he was on his way to a new job offer in Baltimore but had decided he was not going to the interview. Now that he received the reading, he changed his mind. He would definitely go to the interview. We chatted a bit more and he asked if I often went to Baltimore. I told him that I did not, and the conversation ended. We were both being shy. I wished I had taken his information to find out how he made out. I guess our brief encounter served its purpose. Sometimes I believe we are God's extra pair of hands, just to help out now and then.

Another airplane experience happened again when I was alone. The elderly woman sitting next to me was having a hard time shutting down her phone. I was equally inept at electronics. We laughed and handed the phone to a young lad in front of us who seemed to get a big kick out of showing us "older folk" how to make something work. As the flight continued, I felt my hands warming up. I knew she was having pain in her neck. The flight was hitting some turbulence and she was white knuckling the arm rest. I took her hand and told her that I was a psychic and since I knew I wasn't going to die on this plane, neither was she. She smiled at me. I also asked her if she would like me to give her some hands-on healing for her neck. She was surprised at my offer and gladly accepted.

I quietly said my Reiki prayers and asked God for healing for her neck. After about 20 minutes, she said she felt better. I thought this would be the end to our interactions. I was wrong. After the plane landed, the elderly woman literally dragged me over to her adult daughter, chattering away about Reiki and how I helped her get rid of her neck pain. The daughter was not impressed. She ignored her mother and me! I spoke quietly to the mother, telling her she was going to be fine and she could pursue Reiki treatment or training on her own. I just hoped the daughter would try to keep an open mind. Her mother was a wonderful and special person and deserved to be treated with love and kindness.

Experience has taught me that if I move slowly around my own expectations and make an awareness of my breathing, it is like living in another world. Everything just falls into place. I receive answers to questions, solutions to problems and achieve some level of success in my endeavors.

What a beauty in her baldness. Her shape and
shine elegant before the valley.

During one of our hiking trips in Nepal in 2015, I had requested healing from a local shaman. This was in a small village called Thuman in the mountains of Nepal. I was told that the shaman, or Dhami as they called him, would arrive the following morning and

I would need to pay him 3,000 rupees, about $42.00. The Dhami arrived at 7:30.

He was a small, brown man with compassionate eyes. As I waited for the host to arrange the meeting, I "heard" the Dhami call to me in my mind. I sat beside him in stillness, no words were exchanged. We were called over to two chairs in a small area near the bunk house and bathroom. The Dhami took both of my hands, feeling the wrists. He chanted his intentions into his beads and then walked around me, striking my arms and back with his beads, driving out an "evil ghost." He walked around me, breathing healing breath into my head, into my stomach and back to the front of me to repeat this ritual of striking and breathing in the other direction.

I could feel a space open up around us. In that space was a lightness of peace, serenity, happiness and safety. This space opened me to receive his healing with gratitude. I was told by the interpreter that during the Dhami's chanting, he called in a Deity to do the healing. He told me that during sunrise one morning, the "evil ghost" had entered my body. He felt my wrists again and said that now I was well and would feel better. I thanked the Dhami and he let us take his picture.

This did not cure the cancer nor heal my torn meniscus, but it did give me the strength and courage to finish the day's hike, so I could settle into a farm while the others hiked on. Also, our photographer wondered where he had been that he missed the Dhami's ceremony and my husband wondered how this had taken place under his nose without him realizing what was going on! No one interfered, no one else had even been aware.

The sacred space had been created and kept secret in a place with many people and much activity happening all around us. Somehow, we were shielded from any and all interference. Sometimes it is hard to put into words, an experience like this. I didn't ask how the sacred space was created, I just accepted it with trust.

I have been given so many reasons to accept the moment I am in, to trust events taking place and to find the lessons that I am learning in my successes and failures. One example of embracing the situation I am experiencing without fear or anger happened the day I got run over by my two horses. Jethro and Wally are two wonderful horses that we have enjoyed many hours with for the past fifteen years.

Jethro is a large draft cross, Shire and Morgan. He is now twenty-eight years old and one of the most pleasant horses I have ever met. The children in the neighborhood as young as three years old enjoy riding Jethro. We adopted Jethro from Wyeth Laboratories when they were giving away their horses, who had been used to make rattlesnake antivenom. You only had to provide a decent home and promise to keep them a minimum of two years.

Wally was a different story. He had been raced and was falling apart. He was only six years old, a beautiful brown horse with a dot of white on his forehead. When he first arrived, he was very excitable and couldn't stand to be alone. He was very herd-bound.

During his first week with us, he jumped over the four-foot fence that was around our paddock and galloped around our ten acre pasture. He stopped in front of me and snorted several times in my face, clearly trying to tell me something. It was then that I noticed that he had a large chunk of flesh bit out of his rump. I grounded Jethro to his stall for a week. The horses could see each other, but there was a wooden half door separating them. I had a long talk with Jethro and he not only calmed down, but he and Wally also became best mates.

Since that time, my horses have learned by repetition and just trying to please. I have taught my horses to take themselves from the barn to the pasture. Sometimes they are in a big hurry to get to that pasture. On one particular beautiful sunny day I was walking beside Jethro on the way to the pasture. Wally had been hanging back and decided to join us in a mad gallop. Of course, Jethro was not going to be outdone by his younger counterpart. He began his own mad gallop to the pasture.

Unfortunately, I was now in the middle of both racing horses. There were steps and a handrail on my left, forcing Wally closer to me. As he came alongside Jethro and me, he shoved me to the ground. The push landed me on my stomach with arms outstretched ahead of me. I laid on the ground gasping for air and wondering how many bones were broken. I was also wondering what the purpose was for this crazy incident.

I stood up and took the lead rope up to the pasture where I could close the gate and check on the horses. Of course, the next day, I was covered in bruises and brush burns. But I noticed one thing different. I had not been able to lift my left arm above my head for the past year. It seemed to get worse and worse. But now, after the accident, I was able to lift that arm above my head without any pain. The fall had given me an adjustment that my shoulder needed. I wondered if acceptance of the moment of the accident made the difference in having a positive result.

In other words, if we accept the flow, we always have a positive result. I know having cancer might seem like there is no positive result. But I could make a list of what I have learned and benefitted from through this cancer experience. This thought process keeps me humble. It also gives me hope. I know we will all pass from this life, but now I also know I have many things to look forward to on the other side.

This morning, someone is telling me all negatives. I feel confused. I challenge this and a spirit by the name of Padre Piero says to me:

Let's not think about this as life and death or positive and negative but as a challenge to find and hold your balance, physically, emotionally, and mentally.

I know some of you will relate to these experiences because you have had some of your own psychic experiences. And others of you feel like you are reading a foreign language because these ideas are new to you. I ask you not to judge but to let that place inside of you that still holds a child's curiosity come forth, while you keep yourself in God's love and light. After all, you are love and light. Namaste

Nancy in the city, surrounded by neighborhood children,
playing with corn she brought from the farm.

CHAPTER FOUR

Finding Your Tribe

"You will know it when you find your tribe. Those people encourage and allow you to become who you are. That's when you feel freedom."

There are those of us, who need to talk to someone who will not judge us and say we are crazy, imagining things, or telling stories. We bend spoons in many swirls, we know about the spirit that stands behind you and whispers encouragement in your ear. We see Angels and Demons. We send you light and love when you ask us to. We may give you Reiki or send you healing prayers. You might feel calmer when you speak to us on the phone. You might feel serenity just sitting beside us. We are the light workers on this planet. Some of us feel like we are aliens or elves or even have a walk-in soul who is borrowing our bodies to help humanity.

But we speak a different language. We talk about moving kundalini energy or listening to what Archangel Michael or Archangel Raphael is telling us. We talk about helping souls go to the light. Some of us see those souls walking through our homes as they are drawn to the light. They come so we may help them onward in their spirit journeys. We may hear the voice of your recently deceased friend and allow that soul to speak through us and even have us hug you in that special way only you and she would have known.

Some of us provide a service in the form of a business using our skills of healing while others simply offer healing to those we come in contact with. We are all called sometime in our lives to help others.

We are a minority in this Western society and we need each other. I am writing this book in hopes that we find each other and not be afraid to express who we are. I hope we may come together and share our gifts of love and healing and learn from each other.

Archangel Rafael once said to me, *"The helping of others will become as common as making your child a sandwich. You allow this helping to become a part of you. It is not necessary to explain to everyone what you are doing. People will come to you when they need you. I will always be available to help you."*. In this life, if we can help to heal one person' body or mind, then we have lived well.

Finding others with psychic energy and an openness to the idea of expanded existence close to what we perceive as our reality, was the tribe I was looking for. It took me well into my fifties to find such like-minded people. When I use the word "tribe," I am referring to a group of friends we are closest to. Perhaps for some people, tribe includes family members who share commonalities and remain active in our lives. It comes down to clarifying who we are comfortable with and why, who we like to spend time with and share our confidences with and why. We quickly learn that as we grow, we will outgrow others as they will outgrow us.

One of the most satisfying experiences in my life, was finally finding a group of like-minded people. This occurred after I had prayed to the "Spiritual Council" that held the contract of my agreements on this planet. We make agreements when we are between lives, so to speak. We chose many events and environments prior to coming here to help our spirits grow. When our lives seem to become just too difficult to manage, even with God's help, we may petition the council to change our contracts from being a victim or perpetrator, to being about the relationship we have with ourselves, to being responsible for our behaviors and energies.

At those times, the people around us who have their egos satisfied by engaging in unhealthy behaviors with us, may find themselves feeling neglected or put off and we grow apart. It is a bittersweet experience. We may love these friends very much, but we may also find that as we grow and change, many of our friends do not grow with us.

Thankfully we are able to change and improve. Our friends may experience confusion and express dismay as we change. They don't like the changes. We might have less sympathy for their problems because we know they are hanging on to these issues that could be solved. We might see them in a different light. The friendship suddenly seems one-sided. The normal give-and-take in a friendship becomes all give.

Mourning the loss of friends to difference can be very similar to mourning the loss of friends through death. We still love them, but it is better to allow some space. At the same time, we learn to accept both kinds of losses. Death is a natural barrier and yet some loved ones will still stay close after death. I have had to ask some relatives to go on to God's Light and accept my forgiveness as I accept their forgiveness.

The ones who do grow with us are who I refer to as our tribe. These accept us with open arms, reminding us of where we belong. In their arms and in those instances, we are becoming ourselves, growing into who we are. Those people allow us to become who we are. That is when we feel freedom. This did not happen for me until much later in my life. When I was younger, I disliked most people, thinking they just were rude and inconsiderate. I got along much better with animals and managed to trade board for a horse by working on a horse farm. Most of my early years were spent with animals.

Did you ever wonder why you felt like such an alien among your classmates, family, or coworkers? So how do you find your tribe when everyone seems so different from you? I was even told by one man that he knew I was from the planet Venus. Well, even if I am originally from Venus, I surely don't have any memories of that place. It was, however, a nice idea to play around with. It even made me feel very special for a short time. But, how do I find other "Venetians?"

I decided to pursue interests like a hiking club and a gardening club, both lifelong interests for me. The people of these groups were not my tribe. How could I tell? I could feel nonacceptance.

I lived what many would call a normal life. I married, had two children, divorced and married again, having a third son. I worked for thirty years teaching children with special needs. I did not make many friends. I had fought the psychic urges all through this time. I ignored the dreams and premonitions. I felt like if I gave in, I would be deemed a crazy person. Or worse, I was afraid I was just imagining the visions.

Somewhere in my forties, I gave in to the urge to join a group of people who met weekly with a man who was clairvoyant. This group was wonderful to spend time with. We would bring food, sing, talk, and then George the clairvoyant would go into a trance and answer our multitude of questions. I found that I could not stay awake for the questions! This group was very interesting, but they were not my tribe.

There was one person in our group whom I was very drawn to. Kitty was our elder wise woman. She had channeled for many people over the years and supported everyone she could. I learned something from her every time she spoke. She was always peaceful and happy. For her, talking about spirit and God were as natural as talking about lunch. Too soon, she passed over and I miss her very much. Don't ever take the people you love for granted.

Sometime in my fifties I decided to study Reiki, so I could offer healing for people and animals. Reiki is a wonderful hands-on healing modality. I learned how to center myself and receive the healing vibrations. There are three levels in Usui Reiki. Each level involves an attunement. My teachers were interesting and informative. I often had unusual experiences during this training. During my master level training, I experienced a multisensory event that other students also experienced at the same time, but in a different form.

One by one we were called outside to receive a sage smoke cleansing. During my cleansing I heard loud rhythmic drumming and saw in my mind's eye a tall, muscular woman dancing to the rhythms of the drums. She was a brown woman with beautiful, brightly colored clothes and long braids. It was a mesmerizing scene. I was in no hurry to go back inside to our group. When the instructor took me inside, the group asked me if the crazy wind chimes had bothered my concentration. I had not heard the wind chimes and they had not heard the drums. When I described what I had witnessed, one of the women said that the brown woman was her spirit guide. These were interesting people, but not my tribe.

I continued to study Reiki until I received three master levels of three different Reiki forms. Now I felt ready to give Reiki to people as well as animals. I had adopted two horses, multiple dogs and cats, and some chickens. I adopted older animals who needed medical help and care. I found that animals responded much more quickly than people to the healing effects of Reiki.

It was during this time that I found my tribe. I volunteered to share Reiki with a group once a week. I would often also get messages for the people. One woman had a dark area in the center of her body. I suggested she might want to get this checked out. A few weeks later she told me that the doctor had found something significant that needed immediate medical attention. I did not like to give anyone bad news, so I learned how to say these things very gently.

These were the people who felt as fortunate to be with me as I felt to be with them. Two ladies in particular, formed a very close bond with me. They were kind, fun and good cooks! They spoke my language. We spent regular time together. We even took a yearly vacation together. They were also very psychic. We had many wonderful experiences helping people connect with loved ones in Spirit. It seemed that our psychic energy together was stronger than when we were alone.

There was one incident that confirmed our psychic connection. Four of my psychic friends had gathered in my home to give me Reiki. We had a healthy veggie lunch and built a fire in the fireplace. We prepared the Reiki table and I laid quietly as we said our prayers to God, invited spirits of the Light and centered ourselves. There is a lovely mental exercise I like to do daily for protection and grounding. I see my body in front of me and begin to see myself adding white healing puffs of white light to every part of my body. The white light replaces anything foreign or negative in my body. I trace my body with the white light first, my arms are extended, my legs a bit apart. Again, this is all performed in my mind's eye. I slowly add the white light to the back of my head, my arms, tracing down through my pelvis and down each leg. My toes are open, releasing all the negativity from my body. I turn myself over and continue this exercise to the front of my body. I take a "mental" bucket, gather the negative ooze from the ground, dig a hole, bury it, fill in the hole with earth and love and hang up the bucket. I see myself cleansed and protected with God's Love and Light.

After everyone had prepared themselves, the ladies placed their hands over me to give me Reiki healing energy. One of the ladies began to play on her flute. The Reiki was powerful enough, but when the flute music began we were all moved to another level. We all had tears, it was that beautiful.

I felt the energy rebuilding my body and creating a new healthy liver. I recognized one of my spirit guides, Do. He had been with me for years, taking things out of my body and rearranging them for better health. I felt my body split in half across my midsection where my liver was exposed. I was told by spirit that I may feel a little discomfort, so they would occupy me on another level.

I could feel myself leaving the present moment in my living room and floating up toward wherever. I found myself in an ocean. As I floated down into the deep water, I could see the fuselage from a plane with people still sitting in the seats. They did not know they were dead. I began to give them Reiki.

I was floating vertically with my hands raised, like an angel projecting healing energy to help them go to God's Light. I could feel these golden rays emanating from me to the people. They saw me, not as me, but as a heavenly figure. I noticed hands reaching down to help the souls find God. One by one, they left the plane and went Home.

Later, as we were talking about our experience, one member of our group told me she had seen Mother Mary encapsulate my body with her being. She believed that Mother Mary had appeared to the souls, using our energy. I believe we were drawn to the souls who were stuck on the submerged plane. I believe Mother Mary appeared to help them go to God's Light. As crazy as it sounds, I know I'm not the only person who has these experiences.

You will know it when you find your tribe. Those who accept you with open arms remind you of where you belong. In their arms and in those instances, you are becoming yourself, growing into who you are. Those people encourage and allow you to become who you are. That's when you feel freedom.

A wild woman, her lover, and their dog.

Journal Entries of Nancy
By Claudia Kirk

Wednesday, April 15, 2020

A hard time up at Nancy's – me holding back the tears. I could see as soon as I went in that she had deteriorated quite a lot since just last week. How could she slide so far in just one week? She is thinner, mentally unclear, perhaps from the morphine. Her legs are more swollen.

She tried to cogitate. At one point she spoke of being 'cognizant'- the next moment slipping again. My heart sank very soon and I had to tell her 'I love you, Nancy.'

Oh so sad to watch her twist in the desolating wind. She smiles a lot though – good old girl. So game even as it all starts to come apart. Oh girl ♡

Earth Day April 22, 2020

Nancy you have gone.

You said to Julian days ago "There's a very big train in here." And he said "Momma that's the train for you, the train you are to ride" and then you said. "I'm gonna get on that train."

He said you were so innocent at the end – like why can't I breathe? What is this pain? Sunday you deteriorated, Monday you were nonverbal, Tuesday morning you had the death rattle, by eight o'clock you were gone from this world.

Today was a beautiful sunny day in April to drive up to your place, just like the sunny April day my Mom died and I drove to Pleasant View. I saw a photo of you smiling in your home, you good woman. You gave me the wonderful gift of Reiki and I gave you Reiki every week for a good long time. Now that project is over.

You went out into the stars during the Lyrid meteor shower. I have a candle and incense burning.

———————

Thursday, April 23, 2020

I remember one time years ago, I came into Nancy's house around suppertime and she had just backed a corn pie. She offered me a piece and it was luscious.

I remember one time when Bart was small and Bart came to me and said he had eaten some pokeberries which are poisonous. I gave him some Ipecac but he had not vomited. I anxiously called Nancy. She came over, cheerfully picked him up and swung him around in a circle in the air until he threw up. She was fearless and resourceful.

The time she took Steve's mother, who was going blind, to Longwood Gardens to see the beauty.

All the many times she went to bat in the local school district for her 'kids'- her students with social/emotional/learning disabilities.

She was so much better than I and she would never I'm sure, let me say that. She righted every wrong.

Friday, April 24, 2020

I have a ceremonial candle burning in a line with three crystals – amethyst, orangey something, and smoky quartz. It is three days since Nancy exited her body.

This morning I worked my way through the box of nutritionals from her sustained quest for a way through. I wonder- do you struggle and struggle to hang on, then go through the gate of death anyway- then wonder what the fuss and fear were all about?

She said her mother came to her a while back and said, "it's nice over here."

Oh but you struggle against don't you, girlfriend? I sensed how much you didn't want to go. The last time I saw you with your wavering mind you were still using your famous moxie to work the puzzle, to make it through alive.

The ironic thing maybe is that you are more alive now than you were in your failing body. All your psychic gifts- what happens with them now? I don't believe that loving energy is ever truly lost. I expect you are on quite an adventure now.

Sunday April 26, 2020

Tonight on the folk music show I heard an old song from the 60's – Streets of Loredo – and felt strongly of Nancy. A story of striving hearts, loss and love, and horses.

I remember that last day her saying the word 'cognizant' and how it struck me, like a bell. And today I read this (by coincidence?) from my Reiki teacher-

> *"The nature of mind, our enlightened essence, is the unity of emptiness and cognizance, in this context cognizant means not fixating on what is perceived ... there remains clarity totally devoid of conceptualization, a cognizance free from holding onto anything."*

Another moment stands out to me from that day as we were talking for the last time. Something I said she didn't hear right and Nancy thought I had said suffering. She said the world again to herself "suffering' – and her voice was full of wonder at it, as if you were holding a stone in your hand and turning it over- trying to figure something out.

At that point she was close to the end of a long journey with cancer, suffering both physically and mentally.

I feel a very strange feeling this Sunday night, as if I am a ghost myself.

Thursday, April 28, 2020

After a campfire with friends remembering Nancy, three memories starting in recent days and going back to childhood:

1. *Women's Day party at Spirit Run, a good number of women are dancing together in the sunny room. Nancy is in another room talking. Suddenly she runs into the room where I am dancing and begins an elaborately humorous dance of primal energy. It is almost like she is jostling me-to take it is a step up and not be so artsy.*

2. *She slept with my college boyfriend Joe. She was down to DC for a visit. I went away from something. She came onto him and he did not resist. I didn't know anything about it at the time. She told me many years later - said she was somehow getting even with me.*

3. *The thing she may have been getting even about was when we were children. Our family had a little more money than her family. My mother for reasons of her own had spoiled me so that I was lazy and entitled. She hired Nancy to come and clean while I laid on the couch. Ouch!*

Thursday April 30, 2020

I read back over my journals and found that I started going up to Nancy's to give her Reiki in July 2018. So I did that with her every week until April 2020. Just about 2 years.

On one level you could be tempted to say that I failed to cure her cancer with Reiki. But I am certain that is not looking at the whole picture. Did I prolong her life? I think so. Did we build together a spirit structure somewhere that is useful in the long run? I think so.

Sunday May 3 2020

I want to write about an encounter I had with a pretty horse just days after Nancy died. I was on my usual morning walk with my dog, just sauntering along.

Suddenly I became aware of a fine horse on the other side of the fence, very close to me, following me stride for stride. I thought to myself 'Nancy' – and I leaned in and gently expressed my love and sadness. Very unusual for that horse to be there at that time.

Monday May 18 2020

I have some of Nancy's ashes with me. Ed gave me some to put in my garden – her wishes. The remains of her corporeal self. It is strange to be here with a pile of grey dust that used to be what I thought Nancy was.

I went through her spacious closet. I felt a bit uncouth to be going through her affluent clothing (she and I had switched levels as far as money was concerned). Ed wanted me to do it, so I picked out things I thought my friends might like, seriously hippie queen dresses among them.
So here we are in my writing room -one embodied, one disembodied. I have some incense going near the orangey crystal. I have this expectant feeling that there must be something important I can say. Either to express the emptiness, the disappointment of not finding her in the usual places – or to somehow fill up this void. Let it be.

The stick of incense burns out and the ash falls on top of her ashes. "ashes to ashes, dust to dust." I wish to plant some of her ashes alongside some glorious colorful Mexican sunflowers that attract the butterflies. SO my dear friend here's to you. May you follow the great bright light of Love wherever your soul abides.

Lightning Source UK Ltd.
Milton Keynes UK
UKHW041828290421
382872UK00001B/37